£14.99

READY STEADY COOK™
for kids

READY STEADY COOK™
for kids

Joanna Farrow

hamlyn

Note to adults/parents

The recipes in this book are designed for kids to prepare and cook on their own but supervised (close by or from a distance, depending on age) by an adult. Many of the recipes involve the use of sharp knives, graters, can openers, blenders and mixers, or involve frying, boiling or use of the oven. Most of the cooking methods have been simplified, but in some cases certain points might need to be explained.

First published in Great Britain in 2006 by
Hamlyn, a division of Octopus Publishing Group Ltd,
2–4 Heron Quays, London E14 4JP

By arrangement with the BBC
BBC logo © BBC 1996
Ready Steady Cook logo © 1996

The BBC logo and Ready Steady Cook logo are registered trademarks of the British Broadcasting Corporation and are used under license.

The Endemol UK logo is a trademark and is used under license. Ready Steady Cook is an Endemol UK Production for the BBC.

EAN-13: 978-0-600-61432-6
ISBN-10: 0-600-61432-8

A CIP catalogue record for this book is available from the British Library.

Printed and bound in China

10 9 8 7 6 5 4 3 2 1

Notes
Standard level spoon measures are used in all recipes:
1 tablespoon = one 15 ml spoon
1 teaspoon = one 5 ml spoon

Both metric and imperial measurements are given for the recipes. Use one set of measures only, not a mixture of both.

Ovens should be preheated to the specified temperature. If using a fan-assisted oven, follow the manufacturer's instructions for adjusting the time and temperature.

Medium eggs have been used throughout.

A few recipes include nuts and nut derivatives. Anyone with a known nut allergy must avoid these. Children under the age of 3 with a family history of nut allergy, asthma, eczema or any type of allergy are also advised to avoid eating dishes which contain nuts. Do not give whole nuts or seeds to any child under 5 because of the risk of choking.

Contents

Introduction
6–9

Lunchbox goodies
10–35

Yummy snacks
36–55

Diddy dinners
56–83

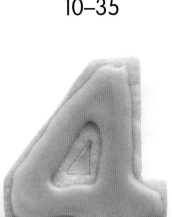

Scrummy puds
84–105

Crazy cakes and cookies
106–123

Cool cocktails
124–141

Index
142–143

Acknowledgements
144

Introduction

Ready Steady Cook kids – this is your chance to push the adults (gently) to one side and let them see just what you're capable of in the kitchen. This fast, fresh and healthy cookbook shows just how much fun it can be to whiz up fabulous family meals, lunchbox treats, yummy desserts and other goodies for the whole family.

In true 'Ready Steady Cook' style, each recipe takes a selection of fresh ingredients and, topped up with storecupboard and fridge supplies, transforms them into something special within half an hour. Some recipes are really quick and easy, and achievable well within the 30 minutes, while others will put you under a bit of 'Ready Steady Cook' time pressure, more like the challenge the TV chefs seem to thrive on! The recipes include some of your family favourites like Easy Peasy Shepherd's Pie (on page 74) and a great sauce for Spaghetti Bolognese (on page 70), as well as some fast food specials such as Fabulous Fish Fingers (on page 58) and The Best Chicken Nuggets (on page 78). The difference is, these recipes are made from scratch so they're far healthier than bought ready-made ones, and they'll show you the essential ingredients of, for example, a yummy pasta salad, super smoothie, or fruity pud. As a result, you'll become increasingly critical of additive-packed 'junk food' in general, and learn to appreciate how to make dishes from scratch. You'll also get to know (if you don't already) some really useful cooking techniques like making a cheese sauce, a salad dressing or a crispy coating for fish. These are techniques you'll come back to again and again as your cooking craze takes hold!

How to use this book

If you're not used to following recipes in cookery books, here are a few basic rules to help ensure that your cooking is fun and goes well from beginning to end.

Ready!

- Read the recipe before you start, then you can ask an adult if there's anything you're not sure about.
- Have all your ingredients ready and measured beforehand. This will save you time and it ensures that you've got all the ingredients you need. Most of the recipes use really basic equipment, but check you've got any necessary tins or cutters, particularly in the cakes and cookies chapter.
- For recipes that use beef, chicken or vegetable stock, you can use concentrated liquid stock, powder or cubes. (Or better still, freshly made stock that your mum or dad might have made from scratch.) Follow the instructions on the packet for making up the stock before you start cooking.
- The main fat used in this book is butter, usually unsalted. Margarine can be used instead, but make sure it is a good quality one, without the addition of ingredients like 'hydrogenated vegetable oil'. Non-dairy fats (such as those made with oil) can also be used, but if you're making a cake or pud make sure they're suitable for baking. Sometimes the fat needs to be softened before use, so leave it at room temperature for a couple of hours before you start, or microwave it very briefly – just a few seconds – in a bowl. Take care though, as it will soften very quickly and you don't want it to melt.
- Use full-fat milk for a creamy flavour, although semi-skimmed can be used instead.
- Fruit and vegetables should be washed before you start, unless they're going to be peeled, like onions and potatoes.
- Unless a recipe says otherwise, all the eggs used are 'medium' size. (Sometimes it doesn't matter what size egg you use – when scrambling or frying, for example, but for baking a cake the egg size will affect the final result, so stick to the recipe.)

Steady!

- Many of the recipes use proper measuring spoons rather than ordinary teaspoons, dessertspoons, etc., which ensures that you use the exact amount needed in a recipe. For dry ingredients like spices, flour and baking powder, this should be a level spoon rather than a heaped up one, so level it off by gently shaking the spoon or sliding a knife across the top.

- Some recipes use baking sheets or tins, sometimes lined with greaseproof paper. To do this, melt a little butter in a small bowl, in the microwave, or in a small pan on the hob. Use a pastry brush to spread the melted fat over the tin. If lining a tin with paper, grease the paper as well so the cake mixture doesn't stick to it.

Cook!

- While you're cooking, look at the pictures to see how things are done.

- Some recipes involve cooking pasta or vegetables in boiling water. To save time, use freshly boiled water from the kettle and pour it into the pan on the hob, rather than taking the pan to the kettle.

- Some foods, like chicken, sausages and burgers, must be cooked through thoroughly before eating, otherwise they can make you ill. If you've prepared chicken or raw meat on a chopping board, make sure the board is thoroughly cleaned before chopping salad, veg or fruit that won't be cooked, or use a separate board altogether.

- Unlike TV cooks, Ready Steady Cooks at home must clear up after cooking. Your family will be really impressed with what you cook, but not so thrilled if they've got to spend ages clearing up afterwards! It's a good idea to start clearing up while something's baking or cooling.

Kitchen safety and care

Kitchen equipment should always be used sensibly so there's no danger of accidents happening:

- Tie back your hair if necessary, and remember to wash your hands before you start.
- Wear an apron and make sure you're not wearing any loose clothing or jewellery that might get hooked on pans, cupboard handles or over the cooker.
- Make sure all work surfaces are clean.
- Clear up any spillages on the floor as soon as they happen.
- Always wear oven gloves when putting things in or taking them out of the oven as the shelves and door also get very hot.
- Make sure saucepan and frying pan handles are turned to the side so they can't get knocked.
- Use a chopping board when working with a sharp kitchen knife. Never chop directly on the work surface as knives might slip and the surface will get damaged.
- If you're not sure about something, don't guess, ask an adult!

Note to adults/parents

The recipes in this book are designed for kids to prepare and cook on their own but supervised (close by or from a distance, depending on age) by an adult. Many of the recipes involve the use of sharp knives, graters, can openers, blenders and mixers, or involve frying, boiling or use of the oven. Most of the cooking methods have been simplified, but in some cases certain points might need to be explained.

Basic kitchen equipment

Here's a list of some basic kitchen equipment which you'll need for most of the recipes in this book...

- Kitchen scales
- Measuring jug
- Chopping board
- Kitchen scissors
- Timer or clock
- Kitchen knives
- Oven gloves
- Tablespoon
- Teaspoon
- Dessertspoon
- Fork
- Mixing bowls

Lunchbox goodies

Crunchy crouton salad

Preparation time
20 minutes

Cooking time
18 minutes

Serves
2

Equipment
grater

shallow ovenproof dish or
   roasting tin

small saucepan

salad bowl

dinner plate

fish slice

balloon whisk

To buy
25 g (1 oz) piece of Parmesan
   cheese

4 thin-cut streaky bacon rashers

2 slices of seeded or white bread

4 eggs

1 large avocado

1 small cos lettuce

Storecupboard
3 tablespoons olive oil

1 tablespoon lemon juice or
   white wine vinegar

1 teaspoon grainy mustard

Method

1 Preheat the oven to 200°C (400°F), Gas Mark 6. Finely grate the cheese on to a chopping board. Cut the rind off the bacon. Put the bread slices in a shallow ovenproof dish or roasting tin and lay the bacon on top. Bake in the oven for 10 minutes.

2 While they're cooking, hard-boil the eggs by putting them in a small saucepan and just covering them with cold water. Heat until the water bubbles, then cook for 4 minutes. Carefully drain off the hot water and cover the eggs with cold water to cool them. Tap the eggs on a work surface to break the shells, then peel them and cut the eggs into quarters.

3 Cut the avocado in half and discard the stone. Peel away the skin and chop the flesh into small chunks. Tear the lettuce into bite-sized pieces and scatter them in a bowl or lunchbox.

4 Using oven gloves, take the baking dish or tin out of the oven and put it on a heatproof surface. Remove the bacon to one side of the baking dish or tin and scatter the bread with the grated cheese. Using the gloves, put the dish or tin back in the oven and bake for a further 8 minutes or until the cheese has melted over the bread and is beginning to colour. Remove the dish or tin from the oven again and transfer the bacon and cheese toasts to a plate to cool – use a fork for the bacon and a fish slice for the toast.

5 To make the dressing, put the oil, lemon juice or vinegar and the mustard in a small bowl and mix well with a whisk or spoon.

6 When the bacon and cheese toasts have cooled, break them into small pieces and scatter over the lettuce with the avocado chunks and egg quarters. Pour over the dressing and lightly mix it in. Chill the salad in the fridge until ready to go.

If you like the combination of crispy bacon and avocado, you'll be desperate for lunch break to tuck into this crunchy salad, which you can make the night before if you like. As well as being fresh and creamy, avocados are full of protein, carbohydrates and vitamin C.

Oriental salad with mango

Preparation time
15 minutes

Cooking time
4–5 minutes

Serves
2

Equipment
kitchen paper

nonstick frying pan

wooden spoon

vegetable peeler

grater

plastic containers

To buy
150 g (5 oz) firm tofu

15 g (½ oz) fresh root ginger

½ bunch of spring onions

10 cm (4 inch) length of cucumber

1 small mango

75 g (3 oz) baby spinach leaves

Storecupboard
2 tablespoons vegetable oil

1 tablespoon light or dark soy
sauce

1 tablespoon seasoned rice
vinegar

1 tablespoon clear honey

Method

1 Remove the tofu from its packaging and squeeze out the excess water. Drain the tofu thoroughly on kitchen paper, place on the chopping board and chop it into small dice.

2 Heat 1 tablespoon of the oil in a frying pan (preferably nonstick) for 1 minute, and gently fry the tofu for 4–5 minutes, stirring with a wooden spoon until it begins to colour. Tip into a large bowl so there's room to add other ingredients.

3 Peel the ginger and finely grate it on to a chopping board. Tip the ginger and any juices from it into a small bowl and add the soy sauce, vinegar, honey and the remaining oil. Mix well and add to the tofu in the bowl.

4 Trim the ends from the spring onions and cut the onions into thin slices. Cut the cucumber into small dice. Cut the mango in half – there's a large flat stone in the centre of the mango so slice down the fruit lengthways on the rounded side slightly to one side of the stone, then do the same on the other side. Cut away the skin and dice the flesh. Tear the spinach leaves into pieces, discarding any tough stalks.

5 Add all these prepared ingredients to the tofu in the bowl and toss the salad well. Transfer to plastic containers and chill in the fridge until ready to go.

Rosy prawn coleslaw

Preparation time
20 minutes

Serves
2–3

Equipment
salad bowl

vegetable peeler

grater

To buy
175 g (6 oz) piece of white cabbage

2 medium-sized carrots

100 g (3½ oz) seedless red grapes

1 red-skinned eating apple

100 g (3½ oz) cooked peeled
prawns

Storecupboard
3 tablespoons sunflower or
pumpkin seeds

4 tablespoons mayonnaise

1 tablespoon tomato ketchup

Method

1 Put the cabbage on the chopping board and cut away the hard core. Slice the cabbage as thinly as possible and put it into a large bowl. Peel the carrots and grate them on to the chopping board using the section of the grater with large holes. Cut the grapes in half. Slice the apple into quarters, cut away the core and chop the flesh into small dice.

2 Add the carrots, grapes, apple, prawns and seeds to the cabbage and use a spoon to toss the ingredients together.

3 Mix the mayonnaise with the ketchup in a small bowl, then add it to the salad bowl. Stir well until thoroughly mixed. Chill the salad in the fridge until ready to go.

Peking wraps

Preparation time
10 minutes

Cooking time
about 10 minutes

Makes
2

Equipment
kitchen paper
plate
small frying pan
fish slice
clingfilm

To buy
1 duck breast, weighing about
175 g (6 oz), with skin
2 spring onions
5 cm (2 inch) length of cucumber
2 iceberg lettuce leaves
2 large soft flour tortillas

Storecupboard
½ teaspoon Chinese five-spice
powder
1 tablespoon vegetable oil
2 tablespoons hoisin sauce

Method

1 Pat the duck breast dry on kitchen paper and put it on the chopping board. Using a sharp knife, cut the duck across into very thin slices. Put them on a plate and sprinkle with the five-spice powder. Turn the duck slices in the spice until coated all over.

2 Heat the oil in a small frying pan for 1 minute. Add the duck and fry gently for 5 minutes, turning the pieces with a fish slice. Meanwhile, wash the plate. Using the fish slice, transfer the duck on to the plate and leave to cool while you prepare the filling.

3 Trim the ends from the spring onions and thinly slice them diagonally. Halve the cucumber and cut it into thin slices. Cut the slices into matchstick-sized pieces. Roll up the lettuce leaves and cut them into thin shreds.

4 To prepare the wraps, heat the tortillas one at a time in the microwave on full power for 8 seconds. Alternatively, warm them under a hot grill or in the rinsed-out frying pan for 1 minute. (Take care when cleaning the pan as it'll still be hot from cooking the duck.)

5 Spread the hoisin sauce over one side of each tortilla. Scatter a line of lettuce, then the cucumber, spring onions and duck down the centre of each tortilla, keeping the ingredients away from the ends. Fold two sides of each tortilla over the ends of the filling and then roll them up tightly from an unfolded side so the filling is completely enclosed. Cut the wraps in half, wrap in clingfilm and chill in the fridge until ready to go.

These fabulous 'rolled up sandwiches' are great for picnics or any day you're out and about. A large chicken breast can be used instead of the duck – cook it for the same time as the duck, then cool and thoroughly chill it before wrapping.

Spicy chorizo wrap

Preparation time
15 minutes

Cooking time
5–7 minutes

Makes
1

Equipment
balloon whisk
small frying pan
plate
sieve
kitchen paper
clingfilm

To buy
25 g (1 oz) sliced chorizo sausage
2 eggs
½ punnet mustard and cress
1 large soft flour tortilla

Storecupboard
¼ teaspoon mild chilli powder
1 tablespoon olive oil
1 tablespoon red pesto

Method

1 Put the slices of chorizo sausage on the chopping board and cut them into thin shreds. Break the eggs into a bowl and add the chilli powder. Whisk well until the eggs are completely broken up. Stir in the chorizo. Heat the oil in a small frying pan for 1 minute. Tip the egg mixture into the pan. When the eggs start to set around the edges, use a fork to push the cooked parts into the centre of the pan so the uncooked egg flows into the space. Keep doing this until the eggs are no longer runny, then let the omelette cook until just set – 3–5 minutes. Slide the omelette on to a plate and leave to cool.

2 Cut the mustard and cress from the punnet and put it in a sieve. Rinse under cold water and leave to drain.

3 To prepare the tortilla, heat it in the microwave on full power for 8 seconds. Alternatively, warm it under a hot grill or heat it in the frying pan for 1 minute – wipe out the pan with kitchen paper first, taking care as it might still be hot.

4 Spread one side of the tortilla with the pesto and lay the omelette on top. Scatter with the mustard and cress. Fold two sides of the tortilla over the ends of the filling and then roll it up tightly from an unfolded side so the filling is completely enclosed. Cut the wrap in half, wrap in clingfilm and chill in the fridge until ready to go.

Giant's sandwich

Preparation time
30 minutes

Serves
4–5

Equipment
bread knife
clingfilm

To buy
1 small round cob loaf, about
   15–18 cm (6–7 inches) in diameter
6 tomatoes
small handful of fresh coriander
1 large avocado
200 g (7 oz) sliced ham
100 g (3½ oz) cooked sliced turkey
   or chicken

Storecupboard
softened butter, for spreading
2 tablespoons white wine vinegar
1 tablespoon caster sugar

Method

1 Put the loaf on the chopping board. Using a bread knife, carefully cut a thin, horizontal slice off the top of the loaf. Keep this for a lid. Use your hands to pull out all the soft bread from the centre of the loaf so you're left with a case about 1.5 cm (¾ inch) thick. (You can keep the scooped-out bread for making breadcrumbs. If frozen, it will keep for several months.)

2 Spread the inside of the loaf and the lid with butter – this is easiest done with the back of a dessertspoon.

3 Cut the tomatoes in half. Use a teaspoon to scoop out and discard the seeds. Chop the tomato flesh into small dice and put them in a bowl. Chop the coriander and add to the bowl with the vinegar and sugar to make a salsa. Cut the avocado in half and discard the stone. Peel away the skin and thinly slice the flesh.

4 Layer about a third of the ham and turkey or chicken in the base of the loaf and scatter with half the avocado slices. Spread with half the tomato salsa. Add half the remaining meats, then the rest of the avocado and salsa. Finally, add the rest of the meats and cover with the bread lid.

5 Wrap the loaf in clingfilm and chill in the fridge until ready to go. To serve the sandwich, unwrap the film and cut the loaf into wedges with a bread knife. Re-wrap the wedges in clingfilm.

Asian sardines with veg dippers

Preparation time
20 minutes

Serves
2

Equipment
food processor or blender

spatula

lidded pots

plastic container

To buy
125 g (4 oz) can sardines in oil

75 ml (3 fl oz) natural yogurt

several sprigs of fresh coriander

5 cm (2 inch) length of cucumber

2 celery sticks

1 red pepper

Storecupboard
1–2 tablespoons Thai or Chinese
dipping sauce

several Thai rice crackers or mini
rice cakes

Method

1 Drain the oil from the sardines and tip the contents of the tin into a food processor or blender. Add the yogurt, coriander and 1 tablespoon of the dipping sauce and blend until smooth. If any bits get left around the side of the bowl, turn off the machine and scrape them down with a spatula, then blend again. Taste and add a little more dipping sauce – not too much – for a slightly stronger flavour. (If you haven't got a food processor, put the sardines in a bowl and mash well with a fork, then add the other ingredients and mash until smooth.)

2 To make the veg dippers, put the cucumber on the chopping board and cut it lengthways into 5 mm (¼ inch) thick slices, then cut across the slices to make sticks. Cut the celery sticks in half lengthways and then cut the halves across into sticks. Cut the red pepper in half and discard the core and seeds. Cut the flesh into strips.

3 Pack the sardine dip into small pots with lids and place in a plastic container. Tuck the dippers around and chill in the fridge until ready to go. Serve with the rice crackers or cakes.

Chickpea and corn cakes

Preparation time
15 minutes

Cooking time
17 minutes

Makes
12

Equipment
12-section muffin tray
sieve
small saucepan
colander
grater
balloon whisk

To buy
½ x 400 g (13 oz) can chickpeas
100 g (3½ oz) frozen sweetcorn
about 10 chives
100 g (3½ oz) Cheddar cheese
2 eggs
100 ml (3½ fl oz) milk

Storecupboard
250 g (8 oz) self-raising flour
1 teaspoon baking powder
1 teaspoon mild curry paste
4 tablespoons olive oil, plus a little extra for greasing

Method

1 Preheat the oven to 200°C (400°F), Gas Mark 6. Use a little olive oil to grease each section of the muffin tray. Drain the chickpeas in a sieve and rinse with cold water. Put the chickpeas in a bowl and mash them against the side with a fork to lightly break them up. Put the sweetcorn in a small saucepan. Boil the kettle and pour a little freshly boiled water over the sweetcorn and cook it for 3 minutes. Drain the corn in a colander and mix with the chickpeas.

2 Put the flour and baking powder in a large bowl. Using kitchen scissors, snip the chives into the bowl. Coarsely grate the cheese on to a chopping board and add it to the bowl with the chickpea mixture.

3 Beat the eggs in a bowl with the milk, curry paste and oil and add to the other ingredients. Stir well until combined.

4 Using a dessertspoon, pile the mixture into the muffin tray, filling each section as evenly as possible. Bake the cakes in the oven for about 15 minutes or until they are risen and golden brown. Using oven gloves, carefully remove the muffin tray from the oven and put it on a heatproof surface, then leave the cakes to cool in the tray.

Cheese and apple scones

Preparation time
15 minutes

Cooking time
12–15 minutes

Makes
8

Equipment
baking sheet

grater

vegetable peeler

food processor

rolling pin

6 cm (2½ inch) biscuit cutter

pastry brush

wire rack

To buy
75 g (3 oz) Cheddar cheese

1 dessert apple

40 g (1½ oz) butter, plus a little extra for greasing

about 150 ml (¼ pint) milk, plus a little extra for brushing

Storecupboard
225 g (7½ oz) self-raising flour, plus extra for dusting

1 teaspoon baking powder

2 teaspoons grainy mustard

2 tablespoons sunflower seeds (optional)

Method

1 Preheat the oven to 220°C (425°F), Gas Mark 7. Use a little butter to lightly grease a baking sheet. Finely grate the cheese on to a chopping board. Peel the apple, cut it into quarters and discard the core. Chop the apple into small pieces.

2 Put the flour, baking powder and mustard in a food processor. Cut the butter into small pieces and add to the bowl. Blend until the mixture resembles breadcrumbs. (If you haven't got a food processor, mix the butter into the flour in a bowl using your hands, rubbing the lumps of butter between your thumbs and fingers until they're blended into the flour.)

3 Add the cheese, apple and most of the milk and blend again lightly to make a soft dough. (Or, if using a bowl, mix them in with your hands.) If the mixture is firm and lots of dry crumbs remain in the base of the bowl you might need to add a bit more milk.

4 Sprinkle a little flour on a work surface and on a rolling pin. Turn out the scone mixture on the work surface and roll it out with the rolling pin until it is about 1.5 cm (¾ inch) thick. Cut out rounds using a 6 cm (2½ inch) biscuit cutter. Gather up and re-roll the trimmings until you've made 8 scones.

5 Put the scones on the baking sheet and brush with a little more milk. Scatter with the sunflower seeds, if using, and bake in the oven for 12–15 minutes until the scones are well risen and golden brown. Using oven gloves, carefully remove the baking sheet from the oven and put it on a heatproof surface. Transfer the scones to a wire rack to cool.

This recipe might sound a bit unusual, but traditionally these ingredients were often used together in cakes, the apple giving a light, fruity contrast to the cheese. Cut the scones in half and fill them with salad or your favourite fillers, or eat them as they are.

Pasta pronto

Preparation time
15 minutes

Cooking time
12 minutes

Serves
2

Equipment
medium-sized saucepan

small frying pan

colander

small, lidded plastic containers

To buy
125 g (4 oz) broccoli

75 g (3 oz) pepperoni sausage

50 g (2 oz) fresh or frozen peas

50 g (2 oz) sun-dried or sun-blush
tomatoes in oil

small handful of basil leaves

Storecupboard
100 g (3½ oz) pasta shapes

2 tablespoons pine nuts

3 tablespoons olive oil

1 tablespoon lemon juice or white
wine vinegar

¼ teaspoon caster sugar

pinch of salt

Method

1 Boil the kettle and pour the water into a medium-sized saucepan. Bring the water back to the boil and add the pasta and a pinch of salt. Cook for about 10 minutes until the pasta is tender.

2 While the pasta is cooking, pull the broccoli apart into small 'florets'. Put the pepperoni sausage on the chopping board and cut it into small dice. Put the pine nuts in a small frying pan and gently heat them without any oil until they start to toast. Shake the pan frequently so they toast evenly.

3 Test the pasta is cooked by lifting out a piece with a fork and cutting it in half. It should be just soft all the way through. Add the broccoli and peas to the pan, stir them into the pasta and cook for a further 1 minute.

4 Drain the pasta and vegetables through a colander then rinse them under cold water to cool. Shake the colander to remove the excess water and tip the ingredients into a bowl. Stir in the pepperoni and pine nuts.

5 Finely chop the tomatoes and mix in a small bowl with the olive oil, lemon juice or vinegar and the sugar. Whisk with a fork to mix and then pour over the pasta salad. Tear the basil leaves into pieces, add them to the salad and toss the ingredients together well. Transfer to small plastic containers and chill in the fridge until ready to go.

Jewelled couscous

Preparation time
15 minutes

Cooking time
2 minutes

Serves
2–3

Equipment
heatproof bowl

small saucepan

colander

grater

To buy
150 g (5 oz) couscous

50 g (2 oz) green beans

½ small pineapple

1 small red pepper

1 pomegranate

1 small orange

Storecupboard
200 ml (7 fl oz) hot vegetable stock

2 tablespoons olive oil

1 tablespoon clear honey

Method

1 Put the couscous in a heatproof bowl and add the stock. Leave to stand for 20 minutes.

2 Meanwhile, trim the stalk ends from the beans. Boil the kettle and pour the boiling water into a small saucepan. Bring the water back to the boil, add the beans and cook for 2 minutes. Drain the beans through a colander and rinse in cold water. Chop the beans into 1 cm (½ inch) lengths.

3 Put the pineapple on the chopping board. Cut off the leaves and the bottom of the pineapple, then stand it upright and, using the large kitchen knife, cut the skin away from top to bottom so that no brown areas remain. Cut the pineapple into chunky slices. Cut away and discard the core. Chop the flesh into small pieces.

4 Cut the pepper in half and discard the core and seeds, then chop the pepper into small dice. Cut the pomegranate in half. Pull the fruit apart with your hands and ease out the clusters of seeds. Separate the seeds, discarding any white parts of the fruit, which are bitter.

5 Finely grate half the orange rind on to the chopping board and mix it in a small bowl with 3 tablespoons of the orange juice, the oil and honey. Whisk lightly with a fork.

6 Add all the chopped fruit and vegetables to the couscous with the dressing. Mix well and chill in the fridge until ready to go.

Light, fluffy couscous makes a lovely change to pasta and rice in lunchtime salads. If it's not all eaten at once, this one will keep well in the fridge for two or three days. You can also add some chopped, cooked chicken, bacon or ham or some haloumi cheese if you like.

Lunchbox jambalaya

Preparation time
20 minutes

Cooking time
25 minutes

Serves
2

Equipment
medium-sized saucepan

wooden spoon

vegetable peeler

grater

large frying pan

sieve

To buy
100 g (3½ oz) long-grain rice

1 boneless, skinless chicken breast fillet

1 celery stick

15 g (½ oz) fresh root ginger

1 green pepper

6 cherry tomatoes

Storecupboard
2 tablespoons olive oil

1 teaspoon ground paprika

½ teaspoon ground turmeric

½ teaspoon dried mixed herbs

150 ml (¼ pint) chicken or vegetable stock

Method

1 Boil the kettle and pour plenty of the freshly boiled water into a medium-sized saucepan and bring it back to the boil. Stir in the rice and cook, uncovered, for about 12 minutes or until it is tender. Check by lifting a bit of rice on a fork, cooling it slightly and biting into a grain. It should be just tender. If necessary cook for a little longer.

2 While the rice is cooking, put the chicken on the chopping board and cut it into small pieces. Wash the knife. Put the celery on a clean chopping board (don't use the board you sliced the raw chicken on) and cut it in half lengthways, then cut across into thin slices. Peel the ginger and finely grate it on to the board. Cut the pepper in half and discard the core and seeds. Chop the pepper into small dice.

3 Heat 1 tablespoon of the oil in a large frying pan for 1 minute. Add the chicken and fry it gently, stirring constantly, for 5 minutes. Then add the celery and green pepper and fry for a further 3 minutes.

4 When the rice is cooked, drain it thoroughly through a sieve. Add the ginger, paprika, turmeric, herbs and stock to the chicken and cook gently for 5 minutes until the stock has almost evaporated.

5 Cut the cherry tomatoes in half and stir them into the frying pan with the rice and the remaining oil. Mix all the ingredients together well and transfer to a bowl to cool, then chill in the fridge overnight.

Jambalaya is a Cajun savoury rice dish from south of the USA that adapts really well to a lunchbox version. Make it the day before so it has plenty of time to thoroughly chill overnight. Instead of chicken you can try prawns, chopped pork or chorizo sausage.

Yummy Snacks

Sugared fruit pancakes

Preparation time
15 minutes

Cooking time
10 minutes

Makes
20–24

Equipment
small, medium and large heatproof bowls

small saucepan

hand-held electric whisk

large frying pan

palette knife or fish slice

To buy
2 eggs

25 g (1 oz) unsalted butter

100 ml (3½ fl oz) milk

125 g (4 oz) fresh blueberries

200 ml (7 fl oz) Greek yogurt (optional)

Storecupboard
100 g (3½ oz) plain flour

1 teaspoon baking powder

2 tablespoons vanilla or caster sugar

a little oil, for frying

Method

1 To separate the eggs, gently tap an egg on the side of a thoroughly clean bowl. Holding the egg upright, carefully ease the shells apart with your thumbs so the white falls into the bowl and the yolk is trapped in one shell half. Tip the yolk from one half of the shell to the other until most of the white has fallen into the bowl. Put the yolk in a separate small bowl. Separate the other egg in the same way into the bowls.

2 Put the butter in a heatproof bowl and heat in the microwave on medium power for 1½–2 minutes or until melted. Or melt the butter by putting it in a small saucepan over a gentle heat. Add the milk and pour the mixture over the egg yolks, stirring well.

3 Put the flour, baking powder and 1 tablespoon of the sugar in a large bowl. Add the milk mixture and whisk well to make a smooth batter. Stir in the blueberries.

4 Whisk the egg whites until they form firm peaks when the whisk is lifted from the bowl. Spoon the whites over the batter. Using a large metal spoon, gently stir the whites into the batter until well mixed.

5 Pour a little oil into a large frying pan and heat it for 1 minute. Add a dessertspoonful of the batter to one side of the pan so it spreads to make a little cake. Add two or three more spoonfuls, depending on the size of the pan, so the pancakes can cook without touching. When the pancakes are golden on the underside (check by lifting a pancake with a palette knife or fish slice), flip them over and cook again until golden. Using the fish slice, remove the pancakes from the pan and transfer to a serving plate, then keep them warm while you cook the remainder.

6 Sprinkle all the pancakes with the remaining sugar and serve topped with spoonfuls of yogurt, if liked.

These pancakes are flavoured with fresh blueberries, which burst during cooking to release their lovely sweet juices. They are also full of vitamin C. If you haven't any fresh fruit, then dried fruits like raisins, sultanas or chopped dried apricots can be used instead.

Tooty fruits

Preparation time
15 minutes

Cooking time
2 minutes

Serves
2

Equipment
foil

pastry brush

To buy
½ small Cantaloupe or Charentais melon

100 g (3½ oz) seedless red grapes

small handful of soft fruits, such as strawberries, raspberries, redcurrants

150 ml (¼ pint) natural yogurt

Storecupboard
a little vegetable oil, for brushing

15 g (½ oz) flaked almonds

2 tablespoons icing sugar

2 tablespoons clear honey

Method

1 Line a grill rack with foil and lightly brush it with oil. Scatter with the almonds and icing sugar. Cook the almonds under a moderate grill for about 2 minutes until they are toasted, watching closely as the sugar will brown very quickly. Leave the almonds to cool.

2 Put the melon on a chopping board, cut it in half lengthways and scoop out the seeds. Cut the flesh away from the skins, reserving the skins for serving. Slice the flesh into chunky pieces. Cut the grapes and strawberries in half, if using these. You can leave raspberries and redcurrants whole.

3 Mix the fruits together and pile into the melon skins on serving plates.

4 Stir the honey into the yogurt and spoon over the fruits. Serve scattered with the sugared almonds.

Late great breakfast

Preparation time
15 minutes

Cooking time
15–20 minutes

Serves
4

Equipment
baking sheet
tape measure or ruler
frying pan
fish slice or wooden spatula
small saucepan
wooden spoon

To buy
400 g (13 oz) sheet ready-rolled
   puff pastry
1 red pepper
2 tomatoes
125 g (4 oz) button mushrooms
6 eggs
8 thin-cut streaky or back bacon
   rashers

Storecupboard
2 tablespoons olive oil
15 g (½ oz) butter, plus extra for
   greasing
pinch of salt

Method

1 Preheat the oven to 220°C (425°F), Gas Mark 7. Use a little butter to grease the baking sheet. Unroll the pastry on to the work surface and cut out four 12 x 10 cm (5 x 4 inch) rectangles.

2 Using the tip of a small knife, make a shallow cut about 1 cm (½ inch) in from the edges of each rectangle, making sure you don't cut right through to the base. Place the pastry rectangles on the baking sheet.

3 Put the pepper on the chopping board and cut it in half, discarding the core and seeds. Roughly chop the pepper and cut the tomatoes into wedges. Cut the mushrooms in half. Arrange the peppers, tomatoes and mushrooms on the pastry cases, keeping them away from the marked rims. Drizzle with 1 tablespoon of the oil and bake in the oven for 15–20 minutes until the pastry is well risen and golden.

4 While the pastry cases are baking, beat the eggs in a bowl with a pinch of salt. Cut the rind off the bacon, if it hasn't been removed already. Heat the remaining oil in a frying pan and gently fry the bacon for about 2 minutes on each side until crisp, turning the rashers with a fish slice or wooden spatula.

5 Melt the butter in a small saucepan. Tip in the beaten eggs and cook over a gentle heat, stirring continuously until scrambled.

6 Using oven gloves, carefully remove the baking sheet from the oven and put it on a heatproof surface. Use the fish slice to transfer the pastries to serving plates. Spoon some scrambled eggs on to the centre of each and top with the bacon rashers and serve while they're still nice and hot.

Croque monsieur

Preparation time
15 minutes

Cooking time
about 5 minutes

Serves
2

Equipment
grater
small saucepan
foil
fish slice

To buy
75 g (3 oz) Gruyère or Cheddar
  cheese
15 g (½ oz) butter
125 ml (4 fl oz) milk
2 thick slices of bread
2 thick slices of ham

Storecupboard
1 tablespoon plain flour

Method

1 Coarsely grate the cheese on to a chopping board. You might need to cut off the rind if you are using Gruyère.

2 Melt the butter in a small saucepan. Sprinkle in the flour and stir it into the butter to make a paste. Cook gently, stirring, for 1 minute.

3 Remove the pan from the heat and gradually stir in the milk, stirring well until the mixture is smooth. Return the pan to the heat and stir until the sauce is thickened and bubbling. Stir in the cheese until melted.

4 Line a grill rack with a piece of foil. Put the bread on the foil and cook under a moderate grill until lightly toasted on both sides. Spread each slice with 2 tablespoonfuls of the cheese sauce and lay a slice of ham on top of each. Spoon the remaining sauce over the top and spread it to the edges.

5 Grill the bread for about 3 minutes or until the topping is bubbling and beginning to brown. Use a fish slice to transfer the bread to serving plates and serve.

Tuna melts

Preparation time
10 minutes

Cooking time
11–13 minutes

Serves
2

Equipment
bread knife
sieve
small saucepan
heavy-based frying pan or ridged grill pan
fish slice or tongs

To buy
2 panini breads
200 g (7 oz) tuna in oil or brine
75 g (3 oz) frozen sweetcorn
75 g (3 oz) Gruyère or Emmenthal cheese

Storecupboard
3 tablespoons mayonnaise

Method

1 Using a bread knife, slice each panini bread in half horizontally. Tip the tuna into a sieve to drain the oil or brine. Transfer the tuna to a bowl.

2 Put the sweetcorn in a small saucepan. Boil the kettle and pour the boiled water over the sweetcorn to just cover it. Cook for 3 minutes and drain through the sieve. Rinse the sweetcorn under cold water and add it to the tuna in the bowl. Stir in the mayonnaise until well mixed.

3 Spread the tuna mixture over the two bread bases. Thinly slice the cheese and arrange on top of the tuna. Press the bread tops down firmly on the filling.

4 Heat a heavy-based frying pan or ridged grill pan for 2 minutes. Add the breads and cook on a gentle heat for 3–4 minutes on each side, turning them carefully with a fish slice or tongs. Using the fish slice, transfer the tuna melts to serving plates and serve.

Naan bread pizzas

Preparation time
10 minutes

Cooking time
10–15 minutes

Makes
2

Equipment
large baking sheet
grater
fish slice

To buy
2 plain naan breads
200 g (7 oz) can chopped tomatoes
125 g (4 oz) mozzarella cheese
25 g (1 oz) Cheddar cheese
25 g (1 oz) thinly sliced pepperoni
or salami
6 pitted black olives (optional)

Storecupboard
3 tablespoons sun-dried tomato
paste
½ teaspoon dried oregano

Method

1 Preheat the oven to 200°C (400°F), Gas Mark 6. Put the breads on a large baking sheet. Tip the chopped tomatoes into a bowl and mix in the tomato paste and half the oregano. Spread the mixture almost to the edges of the breads.

2 Thinly slice the mozzarella and coarsely grate the Cheddar on to a chopping board.

3 Arrange the mozzarella slices over the tomatoes and scatter with the Cheddar. Arrange the pepperoni or salami and the olives, if using, on top. Sprinkle with the remaining oregano.

4 Bake the pizzas in the oven for 10–15 minutes until the cheeses have melted and are beginning to colour. Using oven gloves, carefully remove the baking sheet from the oven and put it on a heatproof surface. Use a fish slice to transfer the pizzas to serving plates.

Beanfeast

Preparation time
10 minutes

Cooking time
about 15 minutes

Serves
4

Equipment
heatproof bowl
sieve
medium-sized saucepan
wooden spoon

To buy
200 g (7 oz) tomatoes
½ small onion
1 celery stick
2 x 300 g (10 oz) cans haricot or cannellini beans

Storecupboard
1 tablespoon vegetable oil
2 teaspoons grainy mustard
2 tablespoons black treacle
3 tablespoons tomato ketchup
1 tablespoon Worcestershire sauce

Method

1 Boil the kettle. Put the tomatoes into a heatproof bowl and just cover with the freshly boiled water. Leave to stand for 1–2 minutes until the skins start to split. Carefully pour off the hot water and peel away the skins. Roughly chop the tomatoes on the chopping board.

2 Peel the onion and chop it and the celery into small pieces. Drain the beans through a sieve and rinse with plenty of cold water.

3 Heat the oil in a medium-sized saucepan for 1 minute. Add the onion and celery and fry gently for 5 minutes, stirring with a wooden spoon until just beginning to colour.

4 Tip in the beans, tomatoes, mustard, treacle, ketchup and Worcestershire sauce and stir the ingredients together. Heat until the liquid starts to bubble around the edges. Reduce the heat to its lowest setting and cover the pan with a lid. Cook gently for about 10 minutes until the tomatoes have softened to make a sauce. Serve on toast or on jacket potatoes.

Chunky cheesy chips

Preparation time
15 minutes

Cooking time
about 15 minutes

Serves
2

Equipment
vegetable peeler

medium-sized saucepan

colander

grater

large frying pan

wooden spatula

kitchen paper

slotted spoon

To buy
2 medium potatoes

2 medium carrots

1 small parsnip

50 g (2 oz) Emmenthal or Cheddar
   cheese

Storecupboard
2 tablespoons mayonnaise

2 teaspoons sun-dried tomato
   paste

a little oil, for frying

pinch of salt

Method

1 Boil the kettle. Peel the potatoes, carrots and
parsnip and cut them into chunky sticks.

2 Place the sticks in a medium-sized saucepan
and just cover with the freshly boiled water. Add
a pinch of salt, bring back to the boil and cook
for 2 minutes. Drain through a colander and
leave to stand for 2 minutes.

3 Finely grate the cheese on to a chopping board.
Mix the mayonnaise with the tomato paste in a
small bowl.

4 Heat a thin layer of oil in a large frying pan for
2 minutes. Slide the vegetables into the pan and
spread them in a single layer with a wooden
spatula. Fry gently for 10–15 minutes, carefully
turning them over every few minutes, until
they're golden. Line a plate with a double
thickness of kitchen paper. Using a slotted
spoon, transfer the chips to the paper-lined plate
to absorb the excess oil.

5 Pile the chips into bowls and sprinkle with
the cheese so it starts to melt. Serve with the
pink mayonnaise.

Toffee chokkie popcorn

Preparation time
15 minutes

Cooking time
5 minutes

Makes about
175 g (6 oz)

Equipment
small heatproof bowl
wooden spoon
polythene bag
rolling pin
small saucepan
large saucepan
large baking sheet

To buy
about 50 g (2 oz) milk chocolate
50 g (2 oz) firm toffees
75 g (3 oz) popcorn kernels

Storecupboard
4 tablespoons milk
1 tablespoon vegetable oil

Method

1 Break the chocolate into small pieces and put them in a small heatproof bowl. Microwave on medium power for 1 minute. Leave to stand for 2 minutes, then microwave again for 30 seconds at a time until melted, stirring frequently to avoid lumps. If you don't have a microwave, put the chocolate in a small heatproof bowl and rest it over a small saucepan of gently simmering water, set over the lowest heat. Make sure the base of the bowl isn't in contact with the water or the chocolate will overheat. Once the chocolate has melted, use oven gloves to carefully lift the bowl from the pan.

2 Unwrap the toffees and put them in a polythene bag. Place on a chopping board and tap firmly with a rolling pin until the toffees have broken into small pieces. Tip the pieces into a small saucepan and add the milk. Cook on the lowest possible heat until the toffee has melted. (This will take several minutes, depending on the firmness of the toffee.) Remove from the heat.

3 Put the oil in a large saucepan that has a tight-fitting lid and heat for 1 minute. Add the popcorn kernels and cover with the lid. Cook until the popping sound stops, then tip the corn out on to a large baking sheet or roasting tin and leave for 5 minutes. Using a teaspoon, drizzle lines of the toffee sauce over the corn until lightly coated. Drizzle with lines of chocolate in the same way.

Diddy dinners

Fabulous fish fingers

Preparation time
20 minutes

Cooking time
about 5 minutes

Serves
4

Equipment
clingfilm

kitchen paper

shallow bowl

3 plates

large frying pan

slotted spoon

To buy
1 spring onion

100 ml (3½ fl oz) Greek yogurt

375 g (13 oz) boneless, skinless cod
  or haddock fillet

1 egg

100 g (3½ oz) breadcrumbs

Storecupboard
4 tablespoons mayonnaise

1 tablespoon plain flour

vegetable oil, for frying

pinch of salt

Method

1 To make the dip, cut off both ends of the spring onion, then slice it in half lengthways. Slice the onion as finely as possible and put the slices in a small mixing bowl. Add the yogurt and mayonnaise and stir until evenly mixed. Tip the dip into a small serving dish, cover with clingfilm and chill in the fridge until ready to serve.

2 Pat the fish dry on kitchen paper. Slice the fillet across into 1 cm (½ inch) thick slices. Using a fork, beat the egg in a shallow bowl until completely broken up. Scatter the breadcrumbs on to a plate.

3 Mix the flour and a pinch of salt on another plate. Add the fish pieces, turning them in the flour until they are lightly dusted. Dip each piece in the beaten egg until coated and then dip it in the breadcrumbs. Lay several sheets of kitchen paper on a clean plate.

4 Pour some oil into a large frying pan until it is about 5 mm (¼ inch) deep. Heat the oil until a few breadcrumbs sizzle gently. Using a slotted spoon, carefully lower half the fish fingers into the pan and fry for 1 minute until turning golden. Using the slotted spoon, turn them over and cook for a further 1–2 minutes until golden. Use the spoon to transfer them to the paper-lined plate to drain while you cook the remainder in the same way. Serve with the dip.

These 'real' fish fingers use chunky pieces of fresh fish, coated in crispy breadcrumbs, and are served with a yogurt mayonnaise dip. They're so crisp and yummy and full of good things that you'll never want to eat bought ones again.

Tuna fish cakes

Preparation time
10 minutes

Cooking time
6 minutes

Makes
4

Equipment
sieve
small saucepan
wooden spoon
food processor
plate
large frying pan
fish slice

To buy
400 g (13 oz) can tuna in oil
  or brine
½ small red onion
75 g (3 oz) frozen peas
1 tablespoon chopped fresh herbs:
  tarragon, fennel, dill or coriander
25 g (1 oz) thin corn crispbread
  slices
lettuce leaves, to serve

Storecupboard
400 g (13 oz) leftover mashed
  potatoes
1 teaspoon mild curry paste
vegetable oil, for frying

Method

1 Tip the tuna into a sieve to drain the oil or brine. Peel and finely chop the onion. Boil the kettle. Put the peas in a small saucepan, cover with the freshly boiled water and cook for 2 minutes. Drain through a sieve.

2 Tip the mashed potatoes into a bowl and add the herbs, curry paste and onion. Mix well with a wooden spoon.

3 Add the tuna and peas and stir gently until all the ingredients are combined, but the tuna stays in slightly chunky pieces. Pat the mixture down in the bowl so it's easy to divide into four equal portions. Take a quarter of the mixture and pat it into a cake shape. Make three more in the same way so they're all a similar size.

4 Break the crispbread slices into a food processor and whiz to make fine crumbs. (If you haven't got a food processor, put them in a polythene bag, place on a chopping board and tap firmly with a rolling pin until the biscuits have broken into small pieces.) Tip the crumbs on to a plate and turn the fish cakes in the crumbs, pressing them gently into each side of the cakes.

5 Pour a thin layer of oil into a large frying pan and heat gently for 1 minute. Using a fish slice, add the fish cakes to the pan and fry gently for about 2 minutes until golden on the underside (check by carefully lifting a fish cake with the fish slice). Turn the fish cakes over and fry again until golden. Use the fish slice to transfer the fish cakes from the pan on to plates and serve with some lettuce leaves.

Crumb-topped macaroni cheese

Preparation time
15 minutes

Cooking time
15–20 minutes

Serves
4

Equipment
medium-sized saucepan
colander
grater
wooden spoon
hand-held electric whisk
shallow heatproof dish
small saucepan

To buy
200 g (7 oz) macaroni
100 g (3½ oz) fresh or frozen peas
150 g (5 oz) Cheddar cheese
100 g (3½ oz) ham
65 g (2½ oz) butter
500 ml (17 fl oz) milk

Storecupboard
40 g (1½ oz) plain flour
1 teaspoon Dijon mustard
65 g (2½ oz) breadcrumbs
pinch of salt

Method

1 Boil the kettle and pour the freshly boiled water into a medium-sized saucepan. Add a pinch of salt and bring back to the boil. Tip in the macaroni and cook for about 10 minutes until just tender. Test by lifting out a piece with a fork and cutting it in half. It should be just soft. Add the peas to the pan after the pasta has been cooking for 8 minutes. Drain through a colander.

2 While the macaroni is cooking, coarsely grate the cheese on to a chopping board. Slice the ham into small pieces.

3 Melt 40 g (1½ oz) of the butter in the rinsed and dried saucepan. Add the flour and stir it in with a wooden spoon. Cook over a gentle heat, stirring, for 1 minute. Remove the pan from the heat and gradually pour in the milk, whisking well until there are no longer any lumps. Return the pan to the heat and cook over a gentle heat, stirring continuously until the sauce is thickened and smooth.

4 Add the mustard, grated cheese and ham and stir until the cheese has melted. Tip in the macaroni and peas and stir until coated in the sauce, then pour into a shallow heatproof dish.

5 Melt the remaining butter in a small saucepan and stir in the breadcrumbs until they are coated. Scatter the breadcrumbs over the macaroni and cook under a moderate grill for about 5 minutes or until golden, watching closely as the breadcrumbs will brown quickly. Use oven gloves to remove the dish from under the grill.

Macaroni cheese is only good if it's really well made, like this creamy, crumb-crusted version, flavoured with ham and peas. It can easily be made in advance, so it's ready to pop in the oven for supper. If you don't like peas, use frozen sweetcorn instead.

Linguine with fresh tomato sauce

Preparation time
15 minutes

Cooking time
20 minutes

Serves
4

Equipment
heatproof bowl
garlic crusher
2 large saucepans
wooden spoon
colander
pasta tongs

To buy
12 tomatoes
3 garlic cloves
2 small onions
250 g (8 oz) linguine pasta
a handful (about 12 large leaves) of basil
plenty of freshly grated Parmesan cheese

Storecupboard
4 tablespoons olive oil
3 tablespoons sun-dried tomato paste
1 teaspoon caster sugar
pinch of salt

Method

1 Boil the kettle. Put the tomatoes in a heatproof bowl and just cover with the freshly boiled water. Leave to stand for 1–2 minutes or until the tomato skins start to split. Carefully pour off the hot water and peel away the tomato skins (making sure they have cooled down before picking them up). Roughly chop the tomatoes.

2 Peel the garlic and press it through a garlic crusher, or finely chop by hand. Peel the onions and chop them into small pieces.

3 Heat 3 tablespoons of the oil in a large saucepan and gently fry the onions for 5 minutes. Tip in the chopped tomatoes, tomato paste, garlic and sugar. Cover and cook over a gentle heat for 15 minutes, stirring the sauce occasionally until it is juicy and pulpy.

4 While the sauce is cooking, pour freshly boiled water from the kettle into a large saucepan. Add a little salt and lower in the pasta, pushing it down carefully as it starts to soften. Cook for about 10 minutes, stirring frequently to break up any bits of pasta that are sticking together.

5 Check the pasta is cooked by lifting a piece up on a fork and running it under cold water. It should be just tender. (If necessary cook for a little longer.) Carefully tip the pasta into a colander and drain most of the water, leaving a small amount in the pan, then return it to the saucepan and stir in the remaining oil. Tear the basil leaves into the tomato sauce.

6 Using pasta tongs, pile up mounds of the pasta in individual serving dishes and spoon the sauce on top. Serve with plenty of Parmesan cheese.

Springtime risotto

Preparation time
10 minutes

Cooking time
25 minutes

Serves
4

Equipment
small saucepan
colander
garlic crusher
large pan
ladle

To buy
250 g (8 oz) fine asparagus tips
100 g (3½ oz) frozen baby broad
  beans
1 garlic clove (optional)
350 g (11½ oz) risotto rice
25 g (1 oz) butter
4–6 tablespoons finely grated
  Parmesan or Cheddar cheese

Storecupboard
3 tablespoons olive oil
1 litre (1¾ pints) hot chicken or
  vegetable stock

Method

1 Bring the kettle to the boil. Put the asparagus on the chopping board and cut it into 2.5 cm (1 inch) lengths. Put them in a small saucepan with the beans. Just cover with the freshly boiled water and cook for 2 minutes. Drain in a colander.

2 Meanwhile, peel and crush the garlic, if using. Heat the oil in a large saucepan and fry the garlic and rice for 1 minute.

3 Add 2 ladlefuls of the hot stock and cook, stirring, until it is almost absorbed. Add the remaining stock and bring to the boil. Reduce the heat and cook for about 20 minutes, stirring frequently, until the rice is creamy, but still has a little texture. If all the stock has been absorbed before the rice is tender, stir in a little water from the kettle. Check the rice by lifting some on a fork, cooling it slightly and biting into a grain.

4 Stir the butter and vegetables into the risotto and serve sprinkled with the grated cheese.

This is a lovely, fresh-tasting supper dish and brilliant for all the family. Asparagus has a mild flavour that tastes a bit like peas, but if you'd prefer to use other vegetables like chopped-up courgettes, beans or broccoli, use the same amount of them instead.

Creamy chicken curry

Preparation time
10 minutes

Cooking time
20 minutes

Serves
4

Equipment
grater

large saucepan

wooden spoon or spatula

To buy
4 boneless, skinless chicken
  breasts

1 onion

5 cm (2 inch) length fresh root
  ginger

2 garlic cloves

25 g (1 oz) creamed coconut

4 tablespoons double cream

naan bread, to serve

Storecupboard
2 tablespoons vegetable oil

1 teaspoon mild chilli powder

1 teaspoon ground coriander

1 teaspoon ground cumin

¼ teaspoon ground turmeric

450 ml (¾ pint) chicken stock

4 tablespoons ground almonds

toasted flaked almonds, to garnish

Method

1 Put each chicken breast on a chopping board
and cut it in half lengthways, then cut it across
into chunky pieces. Peel the onion, put it on the
chopping board and chop into small pieces. Peel
the ginger and finely grate on to the chopping
board. Peel the garlic and thinly slice each clove.

2 Heat the oil in a large saucepan. Add the
chicken pieces and fry for 3 minutes, stirring all
the time. Add the onion and fry for 3 minutes
until it begins to soften.

3 Sprinkle the chilli powder, ground coriander,
cumin and turmeric, the ginger and garlic into
the pan and fry for 1 minute. Pour in the stock
and heat until it starts to bubble around the
edges. Cover with a lid and cook very gently
for 10 minutes.

4 Add the ground almonds, coconut and cream
to the pan and stir in until the coconut dissolves
into the sauce. Cook gently for a further
2–3 minutes until slightly thickened. Serve
scattered with the flaked almonds and
accompanied by some naan bread.

Better than mum's bolognese

Preparation time
15 minutes

Cooking time
25 minutes

Serves
4

Equipment
garlic crusher

medium-sized saucepan

large saucepan

wooden spoon

frying pan

colander

pasta tongs

To buy
1 onion

3 garlic cloves

500 g (1 lb) lean minced beef

2 x 400 g (13 oz) cans chopped
   tomatoes

250 g (8 oz) linguine pasta

150 g (5 oz) button mushrooms

Storecupboard
3 tablespoons olive oil

3 tablespoons sun-dried tomato
   paste or red pesto

1 teaspoon dried oregano

1 teaspoon caster sugar

150 ml (¼ pint) hot beef or
   chicken stock

pinch of salt

Method

1 Peel the onion and chop it into small pieces. Peel the garlic and press it through a garlic crusher, or finely chop it by hand.

2 Heat 2 tablespoons of the oil in a saucepan and fry the onion for 3 minutes. Add the beef and garlic and fry for 2 minutes, breaking up the beef with a wooden spoon until browned.

3 Add the tomatoes, tomato paste or pesto, the beef or chicken stock, the oregano, the salt and sugar and bring to the boil. Once the sauce is bubbling around the edges, reduce the heat, cover the pan with a lid and cook gently for 20 minutes.

4 To cook the linguine follow step 4 of the recipe on page 64. Check the pasta is cooked by lifting a piece on a fork and running it under cold water. It should be just tender. It will take about 10 minutes. (If necessary cook for a little longer.) Carefully tip the pasta into a colander and drain off most of the water, leaving a little behind in the pan. Return the pasta to the saucepan.

5 While the linguine is cooking, slice the mushrooms. Heat the remaining oil in a frying pan for 1 minute. Add the mushrooms and fry for about 5 minutes, stirring with a wooden spoon until soft and browned. Stir into the Bolognese sauce and serve on mounds of linguine.

Mini beef and bean burgers

Preparation time
15 minutes

Cooking time
10 minutes

Serves
4

Equipment
sieve

pestle and mortar or rolling pin

fish slice

To buy
225 g (7½ oz) can red kidney beans

2 shallots or ½ small onion

400 g (13 oz) lean minced beef

Storecupboard
1 teaspoon coriander seeds

1 teaspoon cumin seeds

1 teaspoon ground paprika

a little oil, for frying

Method

1 Drain the kidney beans into a sieve and rinse under cold water. Tip the beans into a large bowl and mash them against the sides with a fork so they're broken into smaller pieces.

2 Peel the shallots or onion and chop them into very small pieces. Add to the bowl with the minced beef.

3 Crush the coriander and cumin seeds using a pestle and mortar until roughly crushed. If you haven't got a pestle and mortar, use a small bowl and the end of a rolling pin to crush the seeds. Add to the bowl with the paprika and mix well. You can use a wooden spoon to do this, but it's much easier with your hands.

4 Turn the mixture out on to a board and divide it into eight equal portions. Using your hands, form each into a ball and flatten to make a burger shape so they're all a similar size.

5 Heat a thin layer of oil in a frying pan and gently fry the burgers for 5 minutes. If the pan is not big enough, you might need to cook them two at a time. Turn them with a fish slice and fry for a further 5 minutes until they are well browned on the underside (check by carefully lifting a burger with the fish slice). Use the fish slice to transfer the burgers from the pan to a serving plate. Serve in a fresh bread roll, with some salad and ketchup if liked.

Easy peasy shepherd's pie

Preparation time
10 minutes

Cooking time
20–25 minutes

Serves
4–5

Equipment
vegetable peeler
medium-sized saucepan
food processor
large saucepan
colander
shallow heatproof dish

To buy
750 g (1½ lb) medium-sized
    potatoes
1 large onion
2 large carrots
400 g (13 oz) cooked lamb or beef

Storecupboard
2 tablespoons olive oil
400 g (13 oz) can baked beans
200 ml (7 fl oz) chicken or
    vegetable stock
½ teaspoon dried thyme or
    oregano
2 tablespoons tomato paste
pinch of salt

Method

1 Boil the kettle. Peel the potatoes and cut them into 5 mm (¼ inch) thick slices. Pour plenty of the boiled water into a medium-sized saucepan and add a little salt. Add the potatoes, bring back to the boil and cook for 10 minutes or until tender.

2 While the potatoes are cooking, peel and chop the onion and carrots into chunks and put them in a food processor. Blend very lightly until roughly chopped. (If you haven't got a food processor, chop them up by hand.) Heat 1 tablespoon of the oil in a large saucepan and tip in the chopped vegetables. Fry gently for 3 minutes.

3 Cut up any very large pieces of meat, then roughly chop all the meat in the food processor (or by hand). Add the meat to the saucepan with the baked beans, stock, dried herb and tomato paste. Cook for 10 minutes or until thick.

4 Preheat the grill to its highest setting. Drain the potatoes through a colander. Turn the meat mixture into a shallow heatproof dish and spread it to the edges. Layer the potatoes on top and spread roughly in an even layer.

5 Drizzle with the remaining oil and cook under the grill for 6–8 minutes or until the potatoes are beginning to crisp around the edges. Use oven gloves to remove the dish from under the grill on to a heatproof surface.

Sausage and pepper sizzle

Preparation time
25 minutes

Cooking time
25 minutes

Serves
4

Equipment
roasting tin

vegetable peeler

small saucepan

colander

large saucepan

large frying pan or wok

spatula

To buy
350 g (12 oz) cocktail sausages, or chipolata sausages

1 red onion

1 red pepper

1 green pepper

200 g (7 oz) tender-stem broccoli

200 g (7 oz) ribbon rice noodles

Storecupboard
2 tablespoons olive or vegetable oil

1 tablespoon clear honey

2 tablespoons sweet chilli sauce

3 tablespoons tomato ketchup

½ teaspoon cornflour

3 tablespoons soy sauce

Method

1   Preheat the oven to 200°C (400°F), Gas Mark 6. If using chipolata sausages, twist each in half several times to shape into cocktail sausages. Cut with scissors. Put the sausages in a roasting tin, drizzle with 1 tablespoon of the oil and bake in the oven for 25 minutes, turning them occasionally. Once they are cooked, use oven gloves and carefully remove the tin from the oven on to a heatproof surface.

2   While the sausages are cooking, peel the onion, cut it in half and then slice as thinly as possible. Cut the peppers in half and discard the cores and seeds. Thinly slice the flesh. Cut the broccoli into chunky pieces.

3   Boil the kettle. Put the broccoli in a small saucepan and just cover with the freshly boiled water. Cook gently for 3 minutes, then drain through a colander. Mix the honey with the chilli sauce, ketchup, cornflour, soy sauce and 100 ml (3½ fl oz) water in a bowl.

4   Pour plenty of freshly boiled water from the kettle into a large saucepan. Add the rice noodles and cook gently for 3 minutes or until they are just tender. To test, lift a ribbon on a fork, run it under the cold tap, then pinch it with your fingers. It should feel just tender. Drain the noodles through a colander and rinse under cold water. Return the noodles to the pan.

5   Heat the remaining oil in a large frying pan (or a wok if you have one). Add the sliced onion and stir-fry quickly for 2 minutes. Add the peppers and stir-fry for a further 3 minutes. Add the broccoli.

6   Add the vegetables, sausages and sauce to the noodles and cook, stirring, for 1 minute until heated through. Serve immediately.

You'll be kept quite busy making this supper dish as there are the sausages, noodles, vegetables and sauce to think about. It's best to turn the sausages during cooking so they brown lightly on all sides. Broccoli is very good for you and has lots of vitamin C and minerals.

The best chicken nuggets

Preparation time
20 minutes

Cooking time
10 minutes

Serves
4

Equipment
3 flat plates

shallow dish

kitchen paper

large frying pan

slotted spoon

palette knife

To buy
350 g (12 oz) boneless, skinless chicken breast fillets

1 egg

125 g (4 oz) breadcrumbs from a seeded white loaf

Storecupboard
4 tablespoons mayonnaise

1 teaspoon grainy mustard

2 tablespoons plain flour

¼ teaspoon ground turmeric

a little oil, for frying

pinch of salt

Method

1 Mix the mayonnaise with the mustard in a small serving dish.

2 Put the chicken breast fillets on a chopping board and cut each in half lengthways and then cut across into chunky pieces. Wash your hands thoroughly. Mix the flour, turmeric and a pinch of salt on a flat plate. Whisk the egg lightly with a fork in a shallow dish. Scatter the breadcrumbs on another plate.

3 Coat the chicken pieces in the flour until lightly dusted. Dip each piece in the beaten egg and then in the breadcrumbs. Lay several sheets of kitchen paper on a clean plate.

4 Pour some oil into a large frying pan until about 5 mm (¼ inch) deep. Heat until a few breadcrumbs sizzle gently. Using a slotted spoon, lower half the chicken pieces into the pan and fry gently for 2–3 minutes until they are turning golden on the underside (check by lifting a piece with a palette knife). Using the slotted spoon, turn them over and cook for a further 2–3 minutes until golden. Use the spoon to transfer the cooked chicken on to the paper-lined plate to drain. Cook the remainder of the chicken nuggets in the same way. Serve with the mustard mayonnaise.

Supper in a hurry

Preparation time
25 minutes

Cooking time
25 minutes

Serves
4

Equipment
bread knife
wooden spoon
foil
large frying pan
fish slice
balloon whisk

To buy
1 ciabatta bread
small handful each (about 5 g [¼ oz]) of chives and basil
125 g (4 oz) garlic butter, softened
4 boneless, skinless chicken breast fillets
150 g (5 oz) mozzarella cheese

Storecupboard
5 tablespoons olive oil
1 tablespoon white wine vinegar
1 tablespoon grainy mustard
1 teaspoon caster sugar

Method

1 Preheat the oven to 220°C (425°F), Gas Mark 7. Using a bread knife, cut the bread at 1.5 cm (¾ inch) intervals, leaving the slices only just attached at the base – do this as though you're slicing an ordinary loaf into chunky slices but leaving the crusty base attached.

2 Snip the chives with scissors and mix in a bowl with the soft butter. Roughly spread a dot of butter into each cut of the bread. Lay the loaf on the dull side of a piece of foil and bring the edges up over the top, scrunching them together. Place on the oven shelf and bake for 10 minutes.

3 While the garlic bread is cooking, put the chicken on a chopping board and use a sharp knife to halve each piece horizontally. Wash the knife. Heat 1 tablespoon of the oil in a large frying pan. Add the chicken and fry gently for about

5 minutes until golden on the underside (check by lifting a piece with a fish slice). Turn the pieces over and fry for a further 5 minutes.

4 Using oven gloves, carefully open out the foil on the garlic bread and bake for a further 10 minutes.

5 Slice the tomatoes on a clean chopping board (don't use the one you sliced the raw chicken on). Drain the mozzarella and slice. Scatter the tomatoes and mozzarella in a shallow dish.

6 Make a dressing by whisking together the remaining oil with the vinegar, mustard and sugar in a bowl. Scatter the basil over the salad and drizzle with the dressing. Using oven gloves, remove the garlic bread from the oven and serve with the salad and chicken.

Asian noodles with prawns

Preparation time
20 minutes

Cooking time
8 minutes

Serves
2

Equipment
colander
medium-sized saucepan
large frying pan or wok
wooden spoon

To buy
200 g (7 oz) peeled prawns, thawed if frozen
100 g (3½ oz) baby corn cobs
150 g (5 oz) pak choi or cabbage
2 spring onions
½ mild red chilli
100 g (3½ oz) fine or medium egg noodles

Storecupboard
3 tablespoons plum sauce
2 tablespoons seasoned rice vinegar
2 tablespoons soy sauce
1 tablespoon vegetable oil

Method

1 Mix the plum sauce with the rice vinegar and soy sauce in a small bowl.

2 Tip the prawns into a colander to drain off any excess water. Cut each baby corn cob in half diagonally. Thinly slice the pak choi or cabbage. (If using cabbage, roll up the leaves tightly so it's easier to slice). Trim the ends from the spring onions and slice diagonally into chunky pieces. Cut the chilli in half lengthways and discard the core and seeds. Finely chop the chilli.

3 Boil a kettle. Pour plenty of the freshly boiled water into a medium-sized saucepan and bring back to the boil. Add the noodles and cook for 3 minutes. Drain through a colander and return to the saucepan.

4 Heat the oil in a large frying pan (or wok if you have one) for 1 minute. Add the spring onions and chilli and fry for 1 minute, stirring with a wooden spoon. Add the pak choi or cabbage and the corn and fry for a further 2–3 minutes until the vegetables are softened.

5 Tip the noodles, prawns and sauce into the pan and cook, stirring gently, over a gentle heat until the ingredients are mixed together and hot. Serve immediately.

Scrummy puds

Toffee noffi bananas

Preparation time
10 minutes

Cooking time
about 20 minutes

Serves
4

Equipment
shallow baking dish
small, heavy-based saucepan
wooden spoon
fish slice

To buy
4 bananas
75 g (3 oz) unsalted butter
175 g (6 oz) can evaporated milk
4 tablespoons Greek yogurt or
  double cream

Storecupboard
125 g (4 oz) light muscovado sugar

Method

1 Preheat the oven to 200°C (400°F), Gas Mark 6. Put the bananas in a shallow baking dish and bake in the oven for about 20 minutes or until they have turned dark brown. (If the bananas are quite large, or not quite ripe, they might take a little longer.)

2 While the bananas are cooking, cut the butter into small pieces and put them in a small, heavy-based saucepan with the sugar. Heat very gently, stirring with a wooden spoon until the sugar has dissolved and no gritty bits are left in the base of the pan.

3 Bring the mixture to the boil, without stirring, and cook for 2–3 minutes or until it is thickened. Remove the pan from the heat and leave for 2 minutes.

4 Pour the evaporated milk into the pan and stir it in gently. Return the pan to the heat and cook gently, stirring, for 1–2 minutes until the sauce is smooth and glossy.

5 Using oven gloves, remove the baking dish from the oven and put it on a heatproof surface. Use a fish slice to carefully transfer the bananas to serving plates. Make a slit along each one with a knife and open out the skins slightly. Pour over the sauce and swirl in a little yogurt or cream before serving.

Sticky glazed fruit kebabs

Preparation time
20 minutes

Cooking time
8–10 minutes

Serves
4

Equipment
grater
small saucepan
4 long wooden skewers
foil
pastry brush

To buy
25 g (1 oz) unsalted butter
1 apple or pear
4 apricots or red plums
2 kiwi fruit
1 large banana

Storecupboard
1 piece of stem ginger from a jar
4 tablespoons maple syrup

Method

1 Preheat the grill to its highest setting. To make the glaze, finely grate the piece of ginger on to a chopping board. Melt the butter in a small saucepan and stir in the ginger and maple syrup until well mixed.

2 Soak 4 wooden skewers in cold water while preparing the fruit. (This helps prevent the wood from charring under the grill.)

3 Cut the apple or pear into quarters and cut away the core. Cut each quarter into two or three chunky pieces. Cut the apricots or plums in half and discard the stones. Peel the kiwi fruit and cut it into 4 chunky pieces. Cut the banana into chunky pieces.

4 Carefully thread the fruits on to the skewers. Line a grill rack with foil, making a slight rim around the edges to collect any juices. Place the kebabs on the foil, brush with a little of the glaze and put the rack under a moderate grill. Cook the kebabs for 8–10 minutes, turning them frequently and brushing with more glaze. Serve the kebabs with any leftover glaze and cooking juices that have collected on the foil.

Cherry dip with sugared tortillas

Preparation time
15 minutes

Cooking time
about 10 minutes

Serves
3–4

Equipment
small saucepan
wooden spoon
flat plate
kitchen paper
large frying pan
slotted spoon

To buy
400 g (13 oz) fresh red cherries
2 soft flour tortillas
4 tablespoons natural yogurt

Storecupboard
4 tablespoons caster sugar
2 teaspoons cornflour
½ teaspoon ground mixed spice
a little oil, for frying

Method

1 Cut the cherries in half, discarding the stones. Put the cherries in a small saucepan with 1 tablespoon of the sugar and 4 tablespoons water. Cook over a gentle heat for about 5 minutes until the cherries are soft and very juicy.

2 Blend the cornflour in a small bowl or cup with 2 tablespoons water and add to the pan. Cook, stirring with a wooden spoon, until the juices are bubbling and thickened. Tip into a bowl and leave to stand while you make the tortillas.

3 Mix the remaining sugar with the mixed spice. Line a plate with a double thickness of kitchen paper. Cut each tortilla into 8 wedges. (This is easiest done with scissors.)

4 Heat some oil in a large frying pan to a depth of about 1 cm (½ inch) until a tiny piece of tortilla sizzles on the surface. Add about a third of the tortilla wedges and fry gently on one side for 1–1½ minutes until pale golden. Use a slotted spoon to transfer them to the paper-lined plate to drain, while you fry the remainder. Toss all the tortillas in the spicy sugar.

5 Swirl the yogurt into the cherry mixture and serve with the tortillas.

Berried treasures

Preparation time
15 minutes

Serves
4

Equipment
potato peeler
small heatproof bowl
3 bowls
food processor or blender
sieve
hand-held electric whisk

To buy
100 g (3½ oz) white chocolate
2 tablespoons milk
150 ml (¼ pint) carton double cream
150 g (5 oz) blackberries
1 egg white

Storecupboard
1 tablespoon clear honey

Method

1   Break off a quarter of the white chocolate. Using a potato peeler, shave off some chocolate curls (enough to sprinkle a little over 4 desserts). If the chocolate is too hard and won't pare off, pop it on a plate in the microwave and heat on full power for about 15 seconds then try again. (You might need to microwave it again, but not too much or the chocolate will start to melt.) If you haven't got a microwave, put the chocolate in a warm place to soften up a little.

2   Break all the remaining chocolate into a small heatproof bowl. Add the milk and microwave on full power for 2 minutes. Leave to stand for 1 minute then stir. If lumps remain, microwave again for a further 30 seconds until melted. (If you don't have a microwave, put the chocolate and milk in a small heatproof bowl and rest it over a small saucepan of gently simmering water, set over the lowest heat. Make sure the base of the bowl isn't in contact with the water or the chocolate will overheat. Once the chocolate has melted, use oven gloves to carefully lift the bowl from the pan.) Stir in the cream and pour into a cool bowl. Pop the bowl in the freezer for 5 minutes to speed up chilling.

3   Reserve 4 blackberries and blend the remainder in a food processor or blender with the honey until puréed. Turn into a sieve over a bowl and press the purée through with the back of a dessertspoon to extract the seeds. (If you haven't got a food processor, you can rub the fruit through a sieve into a bowl and then stir in the honey.)

4   In a thoroughly clean bowl, whisk the egg white until it stands in soft peaks when the whisk is lifted from the bowl.

5   Remove the chocolate cream from the freezer and whisk until it starts to thicken. This might take a few minutes. Once it starts to thicken, gently stir in the egg white. Spoon half the mixture into 4 small serving dishes or cups and spoon over the fruit purée. Top with the remaining chocolate mixture and give each a light stir with the handle end of a teaspoon so you can see a swirl of the blackberry purée. Decorate with the reserved berries and chocolate curls and chill until ready to serve.

These little puds look really professional, spooned into little cups

and decorated with extra berries and chocolate curls, and will keep

well in the fridge if you want to make them for a special occasion.

Serve with bought or homemade buttery shortbread biscuits.

Ready steady crumble

Preparation time
15 minutes

Cooking time
10 minutes

Serves
4

Equipment
polythene bag

rolling pin

small saucepan

medium-sized saucepan

cup

shallow heatproof dish

sieve or tea strainer

To buy
125 g (4 oz) gingernut biscuits

40 g (1½ oz) unsalted butter

250 g (8 oz) strawberries

375 g (12 oz) rhubarb

Storecupboard
50 g (2 oz) ground almonds

75 g (3 oz) golden caster sugar

2 teaspoons cornflour

2 tablespoons flaked almonds,
    to decorate

icing sugar, to sprinkle

Method

1 Put the gingernut biscuits in a polythene bag on a chopping board. Tap with a rolling pin until the biscuits break into small pieces. Keep tapping the biscuits until they have broken into fine crumbs. Melt the butter in a small saucepan and stir in the ground almonds, then the biscuit crumbs and 2 tablespoons of the sugar. Remove the pan from the heat.

2 Hull the strawberries (remove the green stalks) and cut any larger ones in half. Trim the ends from the rhubarb and cut the fruit into 1.5 cm (¾ inch) lengths.

3 Put the rhubarb in a medium-sized saucepan with the remaining sugar and 2 tablespoons water and cover with a lid. Cook gently for 3–5 minutes until the rhubarb is soft but not falling apart. You don't want it to be cooked to a mush.

4 Blend the cornflour with 2 tablespoons water in a cup and stir into the rhubarb with the strawberries. Heat for about 2 minutes until the juices have thickened.

5 Turn the mixture into a shallow heatproof dish and sprinkle with the gingernut mixture and flaked almonds. Cook under a moderate grill for 2–3 minutes, watching closely, until the almonds are lightly toasted and the crumble topping is beginning to brown. Using oven gloves, remove the dish from under the grill and put it on a heatproof surface. Sprinkle with a little icing sugar through a small sieve (a tea strainer is ideal) and serve.

Warm plum sundaes

Preparation time
20 minutes

Cooking time
8 minutes

Serves
4

Equipment
small saucepan
sieve
4 heatproof bowls
balloon whisk
wooden spoon

To buy
500 g (1 lb) red plums
3 egg yolks
250 ml (8 fl oz) milk
150 ml (¼ pint) double cream

Storecupboard
100 g (3½ oz) golden caster sugar
15g (½ oz) cornflour
1 teaspoon vanilla extract
1 tablespoon toasted almonds
icing sugar, for dusting

Method

1 Cut the plums into quarters, discarding the stones. Put them in a small saucepan with 75 g (3 oz) of the sugar and 2 tablespoons water. Cover the pan and heat very gently for about 5 minutes or until the plums are tender but not falling apart. Tip the plums into a sieve set over a bowl to catch the juices and leave to stand while making the custard.

2 Whisk the remaining sugar with the cornflour, vanilla extract and egg yolks in a heatproof bowl. Pour the milk into the cleaned saucepan and bring just to the boil. As the milk starts to rise up in the pan, remove it from the heat and pour it over the mixture in the bowl, whisking well.

3 Carefully tip the custard back into the pan and heat gently, stirring well until thickened and bubbling. Remove the custard from the heat and turn it into the bowl. Leave to stand for 10 minutes.

4 Divide the plums among 4 glasses and add a tablespoonful of the juice to each. Using a balloon whisk, whip the cream with the remaining plum juices until slightly thickened. Stir in the custard until smooth and spoon over the plums. Scatter each dish with toasted almonds and dust with icing sugar through a small sieve (or tea strainer), then serve.

Saucy chocolate puds

Preparation time
20 minutes

Cooking time
about 12 minutes

Serves
4

Equipment
2 heatproof bowls

wooden spoon

sieve

hand-held electric whisk

large metal spoon

4 small ramekin dishes, or other
    ovenproof dishes

To buy
100 g (3½ oz) milk chocolate

25 g (1 oz) unsalted butter

2 eggs

4 tablespoons milk

Storecupboard
25 g (1 oz) cocoa powder

2 tablespoons self-raising flour

75 g (3 oz) golden caster sugar

Method

1 Preheat the oven to 180°C (350°F), Gas Mark 4. Break the chocolate into pieces and put them in a heatproof bowl with the butter. Microwave on full power for 2 minutes, then leave to stand for 1 minute. Give the mixture a gentle stir and, if there are still any lumps, return it to the microwave for a further 30 seconds. (If you don't have a microwave, put the chocolate and butter in a small heatproof bowl and rest it over a small saucepan of gently simmering water set over the lowest heat. Make sure the base of the bowl isn't in contact with the water or the chocolate will overheat. Once the chocolate has melted, use oven gloves to carefully lift the bowl from the pan.)

2 Separate the eggs (see page 38). Add the 2 egg yolks to the chocolate mixture and place the egg whites in a separate bowl.

3 Sift together the cocoa powder and flour and add to the chocolate mixture with the milk and 50 g (2 oz) of the sugar.

4 Whisk the egg whites until they form peaks when the whisk is lifted from the bowl. Gradually whisk in the remaining sugar, a teaspoonful at a time, whisking well each time you add the sugar.

5 Using a large metal spoon, gently stir the whisked egg whites into the chocolate mixture. Divide among the dishes and place on a baking sheet. Bake in the oven for about 10 minutes or until the surface of the sponge feels lightly set.

6 Using oven gloves, remove the baking sheet from the oven and put it on a heatproof surface. Use the gloves to lift each dish on to a small plate and serve.

Upside-down tarts

Preparation time
10 minutes

Cooking time
15–18 minutes

Serves
4

Equipment
4 small heatproof ramekin dishes
10 cm (4 inch) round biscuit cutter
baking sheet

To buy
25g (1 oz) unsalted butter
50g (2 oz) redcurrants
2 ripe pears
½ x 375 g (13 oz) pack ready-rolled
puff pastry

Storecupboard
25 g (1 oz) light muscovado sugar

Method

1 Preheat the oven to 220°C (425°F), Gas Mark 7. Thinly slice the butter and divide it among the ramekin dishes. Sprinkle with the sugar. If the redcurrants are still attached to their stalks, reserve 4 clusters for decoration and remove the rest from the stalks. The easiest way to do this is to run the currants between the prongs of a fork. Scatter several redcurrants into each dish.

2 Peel the pears, slice them into quarters, cut away the core and cut the pears into chunky pieces. Add to the dishes.

3 Lay the pastry on the surface and cut out rounds using a 10 cm (4 inch) round biscuit cutter. Lay the pastry rounds over the pears, tucking the edges down the inside of the dishes.

4 Place the dishes on a baking sheet and bake in the oven for 15–18 minutes or until the pastry is well risen and pale golden. Using oven gloves, remove the baking sheet from the oven and put it on a heatproof surface. Leave to cool slightly.

5 To serve, loosen the edges of the pastry with a knife. Hold a dish with oven gloves and invert a small serving plate on top. Carefully flip over the dish and plate so that the plate is the right way up. Lift off the ramekin dish to reveal the fruity topping. Repeat with the remaining puds. Serve decorated with the remaining redcurrants.

Here's a recipe to really impress the family! It looks like something you'd be served in a posh restaurant, but is incredibly easy to make.

The only thing you might need help with is turning the tarts out on to plates. Serve with ice cream, pouring cream or creamy custard.

Ice dream

Preparation time
20 minutes

Serves
4–5

Equipment
food processor

hand-held electric whisk

To buy
300 ml (½ pint) double cream

250 g (8 oz) frozen summer fruits,
such as strawberries,
raspberries, blackcurrants
and cherries

extra fresh fruit, such as
strawberries or raspberries,
to decorate

Storecupboard
50 g (2 oz) icing sugar

sugar sprinkles, to decorate
(optional)

Method

1 Pour 100 ml (3½ fl oz) of the cream into a small bowl. Tip the frozen fruit into a food processor and add the icing sugar. Blend very lightly until the fruit starts to break up.

2 With the machine running, gradually pour the remaining cream into the processor through the funnel until the ice cream is thick and smooth. (If the frozen mixture clogs together and doesn't whiz around, turn the machine off and stir the fruit and cream to break it up.) Put the processor bowl in the freezer while you whip the cream.

3 Whisk the cream until it is only just peaking when the whisk is lifted from the bowl. Spoon half the cream into 4–5 serving glasses.

4 Spoon the ice cream on top of the cream and then finish each pud with another blob of cream. Scatter with a few fresh fruits and serve scattered with sugar sprinkles, if you like.

Baked ice cream

Preparation time
20 minutes

Cooking time
2–3 minutes

Serves
4

Equipment
4 heatproof glass ramekin dishes,
  each about 175 ml (6 fl oz)
hand-held electric whisk
ice-cream scoop
palette knife
baking sheet

To buy
125 g (4 oz) good-quality bought
  sponge cake, such as Madeira
150 g (5 oz) raspberries
100 ml (3½ fl oz) orange juice
4 large scoops vanilla ice cream
2 egg whites

Storecupboard
4 teaspoons raspberry or
  strawberry jam
40 g (1½ oz) caster sugar

Method

1 Preheat the oven to 220°C (425°F), Gas Mark 7.
Slice the sponge cake in half and sandwich
together with the jam. Chop the sponge into
small pieces and scatter into the dishes. Add
the raspberries and spoon over the orange juice.
Press the mixture down gently.

2 Whisk the egg whites in a thoroughly clean bowl
until the whites are softly peaking when the
whisk is lifted from the bowl. Gradually whisk in
the sugar, a teaspoonful at a time. Whisk the
mixture for about 15 seconds before adding
more sugar.

3 Place a scoop of ice cream in each dish. Place
a large spoonful of the meringue over each
scoop of ice-cream and spread it around so that
the ice cream is completely sealed. Use the back
of a spoon or a palette knife to make peaks over
the meringue.

4 Place the dishes on a baking sheet and bake in
the oven for 2–3 minutes (watching closely as
the meringue will colour quickly) until pale
golden. Using oven gloves, remove the baking
sheet from the oven and put it on a heatproof
surface. Use the gloves to transfer the dishes on
to small plates and serve immediately.

Crazy cakes
and cookies

Sticky cereal bars

Preparation time
10 minutes

Cooking time
15 minutes

Makes
5–6 bars

Equipment
1 kg (2 lb) loaf tin
greaseproof paper
medium-sized saucepan
wooden spoon

To buy
125 g (4 oz) porridge oats
25 g (1 oz) desiccated coconut
75 g (3 oz) dried cherries
75 g (3 oz) unsalted butter, plus
a little extra for greasing

Storecupboard
4 tablespoons golden syrup
25 g (1 oz) demerara sugar

Method

1 Preheat the oven to 190°C (375°F), Gas Mark 5. Use a little butter to lightly grease the base and sides of the loaf tin and then line the base and long sides with a strip of greaseproof paper that comes up the sides of the tin. Add 2 further strips of paper to both the ends. This will make the bars easier to lift out of the tin.

2 Melt the butter with the syrup in a medium-sized saucepan. Remove from the heat and tip in the oats, coconut, cherries and sugar.

3 Stir the cereal mixture well until it is evenly mixed then turn it into the lined tin. Press down gently in an even layer with the back of a spoon. Bake in the oven for about 15 minutes or until the surface is turning pale golden, particularly around the edges.

4 Using oven gloves, remove the tin from the oven and put it on a heatproof surface. Leave for 5 minutes, then, using the paper to help you, lift the cake out of the tin. Cool slightly before cutting it into chunky bars.

Chocolate crackles

Preparation time
15 minutes

Cooking time
3-4 minutes

Makes
12

Equipment
20 cm (8 inch) round, shallow loose-bottomed cake tin
foil or frying pan
2 heatproof bowls
wooden spoon

To buy
15 g (½ oz) unsalted butter, plus a little extra for greasing
150 g (5 oz) milk chocolate
75 g (3 oz) Rice Krispies
25 g (1 oz) white chocolate

Storecupboard
50 g (2 oz) blanched almonds
50 g (2 oz) sultanas

Method

1 Use a little butter to lightly grease the base and sides of the cake tin. This will stop the crackles sticking to the tin.

2 Chop the almonds and lightly toast them, either on a foil-lined grill pan under the grill, or by stirring them in a frying pan without any oil until they are lightly coloured. Transfer to a plate to drain.

3 Break the milk chocolate into a heatproof bowl and add the butter. Microwave on medium power for 2 minutes. Leave to stand for 1 minute and stir the butter into the chocolate. (If it is not quite melted, microwave for another 30 seconds.) If you haven't got a microwave, put the chocolate and butter in a small heatproof bowl and rest it over a small saucepan of gently simmering water, set over the lowest heat. Make sure the base of the bowl isn't in contact with the water or the chocolate will overheat. Once the chocolate has melted, use oven gloves to carefully lift the bowl from the pan.

4 Stir the sultanas, almonds and Rice Krispies into the chocolate until coated. Tip into the tin and pack down firmly with the back of a dessertspoon.

5 Break the white chocolate into pieces and melt in a heatproof bowl in the microwave for 1–2 minutes or until melted. Leave to stand for 1 minute. (Or heat over a pan of simmering water.) Using a teaspoon, drizzle the chocolate over the cake to decorate. Chill the cake in the fridge for at least 20 minutes before cutting it into wedges.

Homemade crackle cakes have a far better flavour than bought ones and contain much healthier ingredients. Dried fruit and nuts add extra texture and flavour, but you can leave these out if you prefer them plain.

Chocolate pops

Preparation time
20–30 minutes

Cooking time
3 minutes

Makes
6

Equipment
2 heatproof bowls

wooden spoon

greaseproof paper

large baking sheet or flat tray

wooden lolly sticks

To buy
100 g (3½ oz) milk chocolate

100 g (3½ oz) white chocolate

15 g (½ oz) dried cranberries

Storecupboard
15 g (½ oz) raisins

2 tablespoons sunflower seeds

sugar sprinkles, or other cake decorations

Method

1 Break the chocolate into two small heatproof bowls – milk chocolate in one, white chocolate in the other. Melt the chocolate, one bowl at a time, in the microwave, on full power for 2 minutes. Leave to stand for 2 minutes, then microwave for 30 seconds at a time until melted. Give the chocolate an occasional stir to blend in any remaining pieces of chocolate. (If you haven't got a microwave, put the chocolate in heatproof bowls and rest each one over a small saucepan of gently simmering water, set over the lowest heat. Make sure the base of the bowl isn't in contact with the water or the chocolate will overheat. Once the chocolate has melted, use oven gloves to carefully lift the bowl of chocolate from the pan.)

2 Lay a sheet of greaseproof paper on a baking sheet or flat tray. Put 6 large spoonfuls of either chocolate on to the paper, spacing them well apart. Spread each blob of chocolate to about 5 cm (2 inches) in diameter and lay a lolly stick about a third of the way into each. Cover the top of the stick with a little chocolate so that it will be secure when the chocolate sets.

3 Use the remaining chocolate, plus the dried fruit, seeds and sprinkles to decorate the lollies. You can add swirls of a contrasting chocolate around the edges of the lollies or over the top, make faces, patterns or even write letters or names.

4 Once you've decorated the chocolate pops, put them in the fridge for about 30 minutes until they're set. Carefully peel away the paper.

Stripy macaroons

Preparation time
15 minutes

Cooking time
10–15 minutes

Makes
16

Equipment
large baking sheet
greaseproof paper
grater
hand-held electric whisk
spatula or fish slice

To buy
1 orange
2 egg whites
2 tablespoons desiccated coconut

Storecupboard
100 g (3½ oz) light muscovado
   sugar
125 g (4 oz) ground almonds
100 g (3½ oz) icing sugar, sifted

Method

1 Preheat the oven to 190°C (375°F), Gas Mark 5. Cover the baking sheet with a piece of greaseproof paper.

2 Finely grate the rind from the orange on to a chopping board. Put the egg whites in a thoroughly clean bowl and whisk until stiff.

3 Gradually sprinkle in the muscovado sugar, whisking all the time until smooth and thickened. Whisk in the orange rind, then the ground almonds and coconut.

4 Place small dessertspoonfuls of the mixture on the baking sheet, leaving a space between each one so they have room to spread a little. Bake the macaroons in the oven for 10–15 minutes until they are slightly risen and pale golden.

5 While the biscuits are baking, squeeze 1 tablespoon of juice from the orange and put it in a small bowl. Gradually beat in the icing sugar to make a smooth, runny glaze.

6 Using oven gloves, remove the baking sheet from the oven and put it on a heatproof surface. Using a spatula or fish slice, transfer the biscuits to a wire rack. Using a teaspoon, 'scribble' lines of the glaze back and forth across the biscuits to give a striped finish. Leave to cool before serving.

Like many biscuits, these ones cook really quickly so you won't have to wait long if you're starving! The orange gives them a really zingy flavour. Alternatively, you can use the rind and juice of a lemon instead of the orange.

Banana fudge fingers

Preparation time
15 minutes

Cooking time
20 minutes

Makes
10

Equipment
18 cm (7 inch) square shallow
  baking tin
greaseproof paper
hand-held electric whisk
wooden spoon
sieve or tea strainer

To buy
1 banana
75 g (3 oz) unsalted butter,
  softened, plus a little extra
  for greasing
125 g (4 oz) soft fudge

Storecupboard
50 g (2 oz) light muscovado sugar
1 teaspoon vanilla extract
175 g (6 oz) self-raising flour
1 teaspoon baking powder
icing sugar, for dusting

Method

1 Preheat the oven to 220°C (425°F), Gas Mark 7.
Use a little butter to grease the baking tin, then
line the base and sides with greaseproof paper.
Lightly mash the banana in a bowl. Add the
butter, muscovado sugar and vanilla extract and
beat with a whisk until mixed.

2 Add the flour and baking powder and mix
again to make a soft paste. Turn the paste into
the baking tin and spread it to the edges. If the
mixture sticks to the spoon and is difficult to
spread, run the back of a dessertspoon under
cold water and use it to spread the dough. Bake
the cake in the oven for 15–18 minutes until it is
well risen and just firm.

3 While the cake is baking, chop the fudge as
finely as possible. Using oven gloves, remove
the cake from the oven and put it on a heatproof
surface. Scatter with the chopped fudge.
Carefully press the fudge into the sponge and,
using gloves, return the cake to the oven for a
further 2 minutes.

4 Using oven gloves, remove the cake from the
oven and, using a sieve or tea strainer, dust it
with icing sugar. Leave to cool before cutting
into fingers.

Baby carrot cakes

Preparation time
15 minutes

Cooking time
15 minutes

Makes
12

Equipment
vegetable peeler

grater

hand-held electric whisk

wooden spoon

12-section cupcake tray, lined with paper cake cases

wire rack

To buy
75 g (3 oz) carrots

65 g (2½ oz) unsalted butter, softened

2 small eggs

1 lime

small pink and orange sugar flowers, to decorate

Storecupboard
65 g (2½ oz) golden caster sugar

125 g (4 oz) self-raising flour

½ teaspoon baking powder

½ teaspoon ground mixed spice

25 g (1 oz) sultanas

100 g (3½ oz) icing sugar

Method

1 Preheat the oven to 190°C (375°F), Gas Mark 5. Peel the carrots and finely grate them on to a chopping board.

2 Put the butter, caster sugar, flour, baking powder, spice and eggs in a bowl and whisk for 2 minutes until creamy. Stir in the carrots and sultanas.

3 Divide the mixture among the paper cake cases. Bake the cakes in the oven for about 15 minutes or until they are well risen and just firm.

4 While the cakes are baking, squeeze 1 tablespoon of juice from the lime and put it in a small bowl with the icing sugar. Mix together with a teaspoon until smooth.

5 Using oven gloves, remove the tray from the oven and put it on a heatproof surface. Transfer the cakes to a wire rack and spread them with the icing glaze. Decorate with sugar flowers and leave to cool.

Raspberry ripple muffins

Preparation time
15 minutes

Cooking time
12–15 minutes

Makes
12

Equipment
heatproof bowl

grater

sieve

12-section cupcake tray, lined with
   paper cake cases

large metal spoon

wire rack

To buy
125 g (4 oz) raspberries

50 g (2 oz) unsalted butter

100 ml (3½ fl oz) milk

1 egg

finely grated rind of 1 orange

Storecupboard
75 g (3 oz) golden caster sugar,
   plus 2 teaspoons

150 g (5 oz) plain flour

2 teaspoons baking powder

Method

1 Preheat the oven to 220°C (425°F), Gas Mark 7. Put the raspberries in a bowl and lightly mash them with a fork until they're broken up but are not becoming too juicy. Stir in the 2 teaspoons sugar.

2 Put the butter in a heatproof bowl and heat in the microwave on medium power for 1½–2 minutes or until melted. Or melt the butter by putting it in a small saucepan over a gentle heat.

3 Beat the milk with the egg and orange rind and stir in the melted butter. Sift the flour and baking powder into a bowl. Add the milk, egg and butter mixture and stir very gently with a large metal spoon until the mixture is only just combined.

4 Spoon about two-thirds of the mixture into the paper cake cases, then spoon the raspberries on top. Spoon the remaining muffin mixture on top so the raspberries are still visible.

5 Bake the muffins in the oven for 12–15 minutes or until they are well risen and turning pale golden. Using oven gloves, remove the tray from the oven and put it on a heatproof surface. Transfer the muffins to a wire rack and leave to cool.

These muffins won't store well so they are best eaten on the day

you make them, but if there are any leftovers you can freeze them.

They'll taste better if you warm them through for about 5 minutes in

a moderate oven - about 180°C (350°F), Gas Mark 4.

Malty fruit buns

Preparation time
10 minutes

Cooking time
12–15 minutes

Makes
12

Equipment
12-section cupcake tray
2 heatproof bowls
small saucepan
wooden spoon
wire rack

To buy
75 g (3 oz) All-Bran
40 g (1½ oz) butter, plus a little extra for greasing
225 ml (8 fl oz) milk

Storecupboard
125 g (4 oz) light muscovado sugar
½ teaspoon ground ginger
125 g (4 oz) mixed dried fruit
125 g (4 oz) self-raising flour
¼ teaspoon baking powder

Method

1 Preheat the oven to 200°C (400°F), Gas Mark 6. Use a little butter to grease each section of the cupcake tray. Chop up the remaining butter. Put the All-Bran in a heatproof bowl with the butter. Bring the milk just to the boil in a saucepan. As soon as it starts to rise up in the pan, pour the milk over the All-Bran and give it a stir to start the butter melting. Leave to stand for 10 minutes.

2 Mix the sugar, ginger, mixed dried fruit, flour and baking powder in a separate bowl.

3 Add the milk and All-Bran mixture to the dried fruit and stir until the ingredients are thoroughly mixed. Divide the mixture among the sections of the tray.

4 Bake the buns in the oven for 12–15 minutes or until they are risen and only just firm to the touch. Using oven gloves, remove the tray from the oven and put it on a heatproof surface. Transfer the buns to a wire rack to cool. Serve warm or cold, split and buttered, if liked.

Make these moist little fruit buns for a late breakfast or for your lunchbox. They freeze well and taste really good, split and buttered.

Dried fruit is naturally sweeter than fresh fruit as its sugars are concentrated during the drying process. It will give you energy!

Cool cocktails

Fruit sparklers

Preparation time
15 minutes

Makes
about 6 glasses

Equipment
food processor or blender
spatula
sieve

To buy
300 g (10 oz) strawberries
250 g (8 oz) fresh cherries
1 large orange
quarter of a small watermelon

Storecupboard
2 tablespoons clear honey
chilled sparkling water, cream soda or lemonade, for topping up

Method

1 Hull the strawberries (remove the green stalks). Reserve a handful of strawberries and put the remainder in a food processor or blender with the honey. Blend until smooth. If any bits get left around the side of the bowl, turn off the machine and scrape them down with a spatula and blend again, then stir the honey into the purée.

2 Cut the cherries in half and discard the stones. Using a small, sharp knife, carefully cut away all the skin from the orange so only the flesh remains. Cut the orange into quarters and then across into slices, discarding any pips.

3 Cut 6 long slices from the watermelon and place one in each of 6 glasses. Cut away the skin from the remaining watermelon and cut the fruit into small chunks.

4 Pour the strawberry purée into a sieve over a bowl and press through with the back of a dessertspoon to extract the seeds. Pour the purée into the glasses and scatter with the whole pieces of fruit. Serve topped up with the sparkling water, cream soda or lemonade.

Juice boost

Preparation time
10 minutes

Makes
2 glasses

Equipment
measuring jug
food processor or blender
juicer
sieve

To buy
4 tomatoes
2 oranges
2 celery sticks, plus leafy stalks
for stirring
100 ml (3½ fl oz) carrot juice

Storecupboard
few drops of Tabasco or
Worcestershire sauce (optional)
ice cubes, to serve

Method

1 Roughly chop the tomatoes and put them in a
food processor or blender.

2 Cut the oranges in half and squeeze the juice.
Add the juice to the processor with as much pulp
as you can scrape from the skins. Finely chop
the celery stalks and add to the processor. Blend
until smooth.

3 Press the pulp from the processor through a
sieve set over a bowl or jug to catch the juice.
Use the back of a spoon to squeeze out as
much juice as possible.

4 Stir the carrot juice into the strained juice. Stir
in a few drops of Tabasco or Worcestershire
sauce if you want a slightly peppery flavour.
Pour the juice over ice cubes in glasses and
serve with leafy celery stalk stirrers.

Golden wonder

Preparation time
10 minutes

Makes
2 glasses

Equipment
plate

food processor or blender

spatula

sieve

To buy
3 yellow plums or apricots

1 large nectarine or peach

2 passion fruit

150 ml (¼ pint) freshly pressed apple juice

Storecupboard
2 tablespoons golden caster sugar

1 teaspoon clear honey or maple syrup

Method

1 Sprinkle the sugar on to a plate. Using your finger, wipe the rim of the glasses with a little honey or maple syrup. Press the syrupy rim of each glass into the sugar, one at a time, and lift away so they're coated in sugar.

2 Cut the plums or apricots in half and discard the stones. Cut the nectarine or peach in half and discard the stone. (If you don't like the skins, peel the fruit before you start.)

3 Put the fruits in a food processor or blender and blend until smooth. If any bits get left around the side of the bowl, turn off the machine and scrape them down with a spatula, then blend again.

4 Cut the passion fruit in half and scoop out the pulp. If you don't like the seeds (which look pretty, but are very hard), strain the pulp through a sieve to extract them. Add the passion fruit and apple juice to the processor and blend again until smooth.

5 Carefully pour the juice into the glasses so you don't spoil the sugared rims.

Peaches and cream thickshake

Preparation time
5 minutes

Makes
1 glass

Equipment
food processor or blender
spatula
ice-cream scoop

To buy
1 large peach
2 scoops vanilla ice cream
50 ml (2 fl oz) milk
few raspberries, to decorate

Storecupboard
½ teaspooon icing sugar
long finger biscuits, such as
    sponge fingers

Method

1 Cut the peach in half and discard the stone. (If you don't like the skin, peel the fruit before you start.) Thickly slice the fruit and reserve a couple of slices for decoration.

2 Put the rest in a food processor or blender and blend until smooth. If any bits get left around the side of the bowl, turn off the machine and scrape them down with a spatula, then blend again to make a smooth purée.

3 Add the ice cream and the milk and blend again until smooth. Check the sweetness and add the icing sugar if necessary. Pour the shake into a glass and gently press a couple of biscuits into the top. Decorate with the reserved peaches and the raspberries to serve.

Black beauty

Preparation time
10 minutes

Makes
2 glasses

Equipment
food processor or blender

spatula

To buy
150 g (5 oz) blackcurrants or
blackberries

150 g (5 oz) raspberry or blackberry
sorbet

150 ml (¼ pint) natural yogurt

4 tablespoons single cream

Storecupboard
2 tablespoons clear honey

1 teaspoon vanilla extract

Method

1 If using blackcurrants, remove any stray stalks.
Reserve a few pieces of fruit for decoration. Put
the rest in a food processor or blender and
blend until smooth. If any bits get left around
the side of the bowl, turn off the machine and
scrape them down with a spatula, then blend
again. Add the sorbet and blend again until
combined. Spoon into 2 glasses.

2 Put the yogurt in a bowl and stir in the cream,
honey and vanilla extract until evenly combined.
Spoon over the fruit mixture and serve
decorated with the reserved fruit.

Two smoothies

Preparation time
15 minutes

Makes
2 large glasses

Equipment
food processor or blender

spatula

To buy
200 g (7 oz) strawberries

1 large banana

1 tablespoon lime or lemon juice

200 g (7 oz) fresh apricots

1 large orange

Storecupboard
½ teaspoon vanilla extract

1 teaspoon icing sugar

Method

1 Hull the strawberries (remove the green stalks) and then put in a food processor or blender. Chop the banana and add to the blender with the lime or lemon juice. Blend until smooth. If any bits get left around the side of the bowl, turn off the machine and scrape them down with a spatula, then blend again and pour into a tall glass.

2 Cut the apricots in half and discard the stones. Wash the processor bowl and blade and add the apricots. Cut the orange in half and squeeze the juice. Add the juice to the processor with the vanilla extract. Blend until smooth. If any bits get left around the side of the bowl, turn off the machine and scrape them down with a spatula, then blend again. Check the sweetness. You might like to add a little icing sugar. Pour the smoothie into another tall glass and serve.

Ready steady go!

Preparation time
15 minutes

Makes
2 glasses

Equipment
food processor or blender

spatula

sieve

straws or long spoons

To buy
3 kiwi fruit

150 ml (¼ pint) pot tangy flavoured
    yogurt, such as lemon or orange

1 small mango

2 tablespoons orange or apple
    juice

150 g (5 oz) raspberries

Storecupboard
1–2 teaspoons clear honey

Method

1 Peel the kiwi fruit and roughly chop the flesh.
   Whiz in a food processor or blender until
   smooth. If any bits get left around the side of the
   bowl, turn off the machine and scrape them
   down with a spatula, then blend again.

2 Spoon the kiwi mixture into the bases of two tall
   glasses. Top each with a spoonful of yogurt,
   spreading the yogurt around the sides of the
   glasses with a teaspoon to create a layered
   effect. Wash the processor bowl and blade.

3 Cut the mango in half – there's a large flat stone
   in the centre so slice down the fruit lengthways
   on the rounded side slightly to one side of it,
   then do the same on the other side. Cut away
   the skin and dice the flesh. Blend to a purée with
   the orange or apple juice, as above, and spoon
   into the glasses. Top with another layer of
   yogurt. Wash the bowl and blade again.

4 Blend the raspberries and tip into a sieve, set
   over a bowl. Press the raspberries through the
   sieve to extract the seeds. Check their
   sweetness. You might need to stir in a little
   honey if they're very sharp. Spoon the raspberry
   purée into the glasses and serve with straws or
   long spoons.

Chocolate heaven

Preparation time
15 minutes

Cooking time
3–4 minutes

Makes
1 large glass

Equipment
2 small heatproof bowls
wooden spoon
food processor or blender
ice-cream scoop
tea strainer

To buy
25 g (1 oz) plain chocolate
60 g (2½ oz) milk chocolate
150 ml (¼ pint) milk
1 large banana
2 large scoops vanilla ice cream

Storecupboard
cocoa powder, for dusting

Method

1 Break the plain chocolate into small pieces and put it in a small heatproof bowl. Microwave on full power for 1 minute. Leave to stand for 1 minute, then microwave for 30 seconds at a time until the chocolate is soft. (If you haven't got a microwave, put the chocolate in a small heatproof bowl and rest it over a small saucepan of gently simmering water, set over the lowest heat. Make sure the base of the bowl isn't in contact with the water or the chocolate will overheat. Once the chocolate has melted, use oven gloves to carefully lift the bowl from the pan.)

2 Break up the milk chocolate and put it in a small heatproof bowl with half the milk. Microwave on full power for 1 minute. Leave to stand for 1 minute. Microwave for 30 seconds at a time, stirring in between each until the chocolate has melted. (Or use the pan method.)

3 Using a teaspoon, make a decorative pattern around the inside of a tall glass with the plain chocolate, either by making little dots of chocolate, swirling it or making little shapes.

4 Stir the remaining milk into the milk chocolate mixture and pour into a food processor or blender. Break the banana into pieces and add to the blender. Blend until smooth. Add one scoop of ice cream and blend again until the mixture is smooth and combined.

5 Pour into the glass. Top with another scoop of ice cream, sift over some cocoa powder (use a tea strainer) and serve.

Index

A

All-Bran: Malty fruit buns 122
apple juice:
    Golden wonder 130
    Ready steady go! 138
apples:
    Cheese and apple scones 28
    Sticky glazed fruit kebabs 88
apricots:
    Apricot and orange smoothie 136
    Golden wonder 130
    Sticky glazed fruit kebabs 88
Asian noodles with prawns 82
Asian sardines with veg dippers 24
asparagus: Springtime risotto 66
avocado:
    Crunchy crouton salad 12
    Giant's sandwich 22

B

Baby carrot cakes 118
bacon:
    Crunchy crouton salad 12
    Late great breakfast 42
Baked ice cream 104
baking sheets and tins 8
bananas:
    Banana fudge fingers 116
    Chocolate heaven 140
    Sticky glazed fruit kebabs 88
    Strawberry and banana
      smoothie 136
    Toffee noffi bananas 86
Beanfeast 50
beef:
    Better than mum's bolognese 70
    Easy peasy shepherd's pie 74
    Mini beef and bean burgers 72
Berried treasures 92
Best chicken nuggets 78
Better than mum's bolognese 70

Black beauty 134
blackberries:
    Berried treasures 92
    Black beauty 134
    blackberry sorbet:
    Black beauty 134
blackcurrants: Black beauty 134
blueberries: Sugared fruit
    pancakes 38
broad beans:
    Springtime risotto 66
broccoli:
    Pasta pronto 30
    Sausage and pepper sizzle 76
burgers:
    Mini beef and bean burgers 72

C

cabbage: Rosy prawn coleslaw 16
cannellini beans: Beanfeast 50
carrot juice: Juice boost 128
carrots: Baby carrot cakes 118
Chunky cheesy chips 52
Cereal bars 108
cheese:
    Cheese and apple scones 28
    Chunky cheesy chips 52
    Croque monsieur 44
    Crumb-topped
      macaroni cheese 62
    Naan bread pizzas 48
    Supper in a hurry 80
    Tuna melts 46
cherries:
    Cherry dip with
      sugared tortillas 90
    Fruit Sparklers 126
chicken:
    Best chicken nuggets 78
    Creamy chicken curry 68
    Giant's sandwich 22
    Lunchbox jambalaya 34
    Supper in a hurry 80
Chickpea and corn cakes 26

chocolate:
    Berried treasures 92
    Chocolate crackles 110
    Chocolate heaven 140
    Chocolate pops 112
    Saucy chocolate puds 98
    Toffee chokkie popcorn 54
chorizo sausage:
    Spicy chorizo wrap 20
Chunky cheesy chips 52
ciabatta bread: Supper in a hurry 80
cleaning up 8
coconut: Stripy macaroons 114
cod: Fabulous fish fingers 58
coleslaw: Rosy prawn coleslaw 16
couscous: Jewelled couscous 32
cranberrries: Chocolate pops 112
cream:
    Berried treasures 92
    Ice dream 102
    Warm plum sundaes 96
Creamy chicken curry 68
Croque monsieur 44
Crumb-topped macaroni cheese 62
crumble: Ready steady crumble 94
Crunchy crouton salad 12
curry: Creamy chicken curry 68

D

dried fruit: Malty fruit buns 122
duck: Peking wraps 18

E

Easy peasy shepherd's pie 74
eggs:
    Baked ice cream 104
    Crunchy crouton salad 12
    Late great breakfast 42
    Saucy chocolate puds 98
    size 7
    Sugared fruit pancakes 38
    Warm plum sundaes 96
equipment 9

F

Fabulous fish fingers 58
fish: Fabulous fish fingers 58
fruit:
    Fruit sparklers 126
    Ice dream 102
    preparing 7
    Sticky glazed fruit kebabs 88
    Sugared fruit pancakes 38
    Tooty fruits 40
fruit, dried: Malty fruit buns 122
fudge: Banana fudge fingers 116

G

Giant's sandwich 22
Golden wonder 130
grapes: Tooty fruits 40

H

haddock: Fabulous fish fingers 58
ham:
    Croque monsieur 44
    Giant's sandwich 22
haricot beans: Beanfeast 50

I

ice cream:
    Baked ice cream 104
    Chocolate heaven 140
    Peaches and cream
      thickshake 132
    Ice dream 102
ingredients 7

J

Jambalaya 34
Jewelled couscous 32
Juice boost 128

K

kidney beans:
    Mini beef and bean burgers 72
kiwi fruit:
    Ready steady go! 138
    Sticky glazed fruit kebabs 88

L

lamb: Easy peasy shepherd's pie   74
Late great breakfast   42
linguine:
   Better than mum's bolognese   70
   Linguine with
      fresh tomato sauce   64
Lunchbox jambalaya   34

M

macaroni: Crumb-topped
   macaroni cheese   62
Macaroons   114
Malty fruit buns   122
mango:
   Oriental salad with mango   14
   Ready steady go!   138
margarine: types to use   7
measuring   8
melon: Tooty fruits   40
milk   7
muffins: Raspberry ripple muffins   120
mushrooms:
   Better than mum's bolognese   70
   Late great breakfast   42

N

Naan bread pizzas   48
nectarines: Golden wonder   130
noodles:
   Asian noodles with prawns   82
   Sausage and pepper sizzle   76

O

orange juice: Ready steady go!   138
oranges:
   Apricot and orange smoothie   136
   Fruit sparklers   126
   Juice boost   128
Oriental salad with mango   14

P

pancakes: Sugared fruit pancakes   38
parsnips: Chunky cheesy chips   52
passion fruit: Golden wonder   130

pasta:
   Better than mum's bolognese   70
   Linguine with
      fresh tomato sauce   64
   Pasta pronto   30
peaches:
   Golden wonder   130
   Peaches and
      cream thickshake   132
pears:
   Sticky glazed fruit kebabs   88
   Upside-down tarts   100
Peking wraps   18–19
pepperoni sausage: Pasta pronto   30
peppers:
   Late great breakfast   42
   Sausage and pepper sizzle   76
pizza: Naan bread pizzas   48
plums:
   Golden wonder   130
   Sticky glazed fruit kebabs   88
   Warm plum sundaes   96
popcorn: Toffee chokkie popcorn   54
porridge oats: Sticky cereal bars   108
potatoes:
   Chunky cheesy chips   52
   Easy peasy shepherd's pie   74
prawns:
   Asian noodles with prawns   82
   Rosy prawn coleslaw   16

R

raspberries:
   Baked ice cream   104
   Raspberry ripple muffins   120
   Ready steady go!   138
   raspberry sorbet: Black beauty 134
Ready steady crumble   94
Ready steady go!   138
redcurrants: Upside-down tarts   100
rhubarb: Ready steady crumble   94
rice: Springtime risotto   66
Rice Krispies: Chocolate crackles   110
Rosy prawn coleslaw   16

S

safety   9
salads:
   Crunchy crouton salad   12
   Oriental salad with mango   14
sandwich: Giant's   22
sardines: Asian sardines
   with veg dippers   24
Saucy chocolate puds   98
sausages:
   Pasta pronto   30
   Sausage and pepper sizzle   76
   Spicy chorizo wrap   20
scones: Cheese and apple scones 28
Shepherd's pie   74
Smoothies   136
Spicy chorizo wrap   20
spoons: for measuring   8
Springtime risotto   66
Sticky cereal bars   108
Sticky glazed fruit kebabs   88
stock cubes   7
strawberries:
   Fruit Sparklers   126
   Ready steady crumble   94
   Strawberry and
      banana smoothie   136
Stripy macaroons   114–15
Sugared fruit pancakes   38
Supper in a hurry   80
sweetcorn:
   Chickpea and corn cakes   26
   Tuna melts   46

T

tarts: Upside-down tarts   100
Toffee chokkie popcorn   54
Toffee noffi bananas   86
tofu: Oriental salad with mango   14
tomatoes:
   Beanfeast   50
   Better than mum's bolognese   70
   Giant's sandwich   22
   Juice boost   128
   Linguine with
      fresh tomato sauce   64
   Naan bread pizzas   48
Tooty fruits   40
tortillas:
   Cherry dip with
      sugared tortillas   90
   Peking wraps   18
   Spicy chorizo wrap   20
tuna:
   Tuna fish cakes   60
   Tuna melts   46
turkey: Giant's sandwich   22

U

Upside-down tarts   100

V

vegetables: preparing   7

W

watermelon: Fruit sparklers   126

Y

yogurt:
   Black beauty   134
   Cherry dip with
      sugared tortillas   90
   Ready steady go!   138

Acknowledgements

Executive Editor **Sarah Ford**
Editor **Charlotte Wilson**
Executive Art Editor **Joanna MacGregor**
Designer **Grade Design Consultants**
Senior Production Controller **Manjit Sihra**
Picture Researcher **Jennifer Veall**
Food Styling **Emma Jane Frost, Tonia George and David Morgan**
Photography **Lis Parsons**
Stylist **Liz Hippisley**

Hamlyn would like to thank:
Linda Clifford Executive Producer, Miranda Lyons Producer, Ready Steady Cook
Production Team

Thanks also to all the children who took part in the photography for this book and made
the photoshoot such a success:

**Luke Adams, Georgia Cowie, Sophie Davies, Khanyisile Edwards,
Charlie Frost, Jasmine Frost, Charlotte Lee, Martha McGonagle,
Thomas McPherson, Eleanor McPherson, Emily Milligan, Jaime Milligan,
Beth Penman, Ruby Penman, Luke Rawlinson, Ashleigh Rossington-Smith,
Aamish Saini, Alfie Williams**

Picture acknowledgements

Special Photography ©Octopus Publishing Group Limited/ Lis Parsons.

Other photography: Octopus Publishing Group Limited/Vanessa Davies 1, 7 left, 7 centre,
8 left, 8 right, 8 centre, 9 left, 9 right, 9 centre, 10, 36 top left, 36 bottom right, 36 top centre
right, 56 bottom right.